Free as a Bird

MICHAEL Q. PINK

Foreword by Ryan Pink

Michael Pink Innovations, LLC

Free As A Bird by Michael Q. Pink
Published by Michael Pink Innovations, LLC

Cover design by Mark Herron of MR Herron Productions

ISBN: 978-1-877994-07-4

For information on our 3-Day Freedom Retreats, contact us through one of our sites...

MichaelPink.com
SupernaturalBusiness.com
Jesus SchoolOfBusiness.com

https://www.YouTube.com/@MichaelQPink

Books & Courses by Michael Q. Pink

Biblical Business

Selling Among Wolves, 7 Secrets of the Sale, Branding, Rainforest Strategy, Taking Back the Gates of Commerce, The Divine Blueprint, The Race is Not to the Swift, The Perfect Business Model, The Bible Incorporated, Christian Wealth Building, 7 Ways to Know God's Voice For Your Life and Business

Christian Living

The Words in Red, Psalm 91 – The Ultimate Shield, His Little Instruction Book, Promises Worth Keeping, Tough Questions – Straight Answers, The Lord's Prayer Amplified, The Comforter, The 23rd Psalm, The Beatitudes, Grace For Grief, The Armor of God, The Rock Student Bible

Co-Author

Profiles of Success, How To Manage One Million Dollars – Or Less

JESUS SCHOOL OF BUSINESS - Training Courses

The Orchid Element, 7 Marketing Secrets From Isaiah, Marketing Secrets of John the Baptist, The 3-Step Marketing Process Modeled by Trees, Natural Law Reveals Powerful Lead Magnet Strategy, How Would Jesus Market?, The 2500 Year-Old Marketing Strategy God Gave Habakkuk. The Science of Selling, The Moses Questioning Strategy, 7 Laws of Persuasion, Motivational Secrets of the Ten Commandments, E.A.S.Y. Close Sales Process, Whole Brain Selling, Negotiating Secrets of the Apostle Paul, The Genesis Business Model, Rain Catcher's Secret, Closing the Sale and Principles of Trust, Inner Court Mysteries, Outer Court Wisdom, Communication Strategies of Jesus, Presentation Secrets of the Apostle Peter, Mindset, Goals, Wisdom – The Ultimate Wealth Creator, The 7 Success Governors, The 7 Proactive Business Beatitudes, The Power of Belief, Natural Laws of Time Management, Rainforest Strategy Course

DEDICATION

For Judy Ann

This book would most likely have never been imagined, let alone written if not for Judy's frequent reminders to me of the promise of Jesus in Matthew 6:26 that if God feeds the birds, will He not also take care of us?

Although I have long believed that at a surface level, when I finally decided to "Behold the birds" I discovered what Judy was trying to infuse into my spirit.

When I needed a revelation of God's love, Judy patiently opened my eyes to that. When I needed the peace of God to deal with deep loss, she is the one who guided me to "take peace" in much the same way you would "take courage" or "take heart".

But somehow this promise of provision always available to me, remained at an intellectual level until I finally took Judy's advice and began to study birds to learn exactly what Jesus meant when He said to behold them or consider them.

It was then, with her constant encouragement and the powerful inspiration of the Holy Spirit, I truly began to grasp at a heart level what it means to live worry free in God's abundance.

So, my darling Judy Ann, I am and will forever be, grateful for you and hopelessly in love with you. You light up my life in ways I dared never to hope for.

Michael

FOREWORD

Dear Reader,

I have been fortunate to have a rare vantage point into the life of Michael Q. Pink, on the content of this book and into the very practical application of the principles within it to the lives of ordinary people.

Long before the first draft of these pages were ever written, I watched Michael live the principles out in his daily life for decades. I watched closely as he has sought diligently to squeeze the mysteries of heaven from the things of earth as a practice in knowing intimately the Father's heart. And I watched, in real time, as those mysteries brought him to a deeper revelation of God than he ever imagined possible.

So much so, I suspect he would have written the famous words "I am merely thinking God's thoughts after Him" had he been born 400 years earlier, and could have beaten Johannes Kepler to the punch.

Although this is just his third book in 20 years to directly look to God's natural created order for inspiration and instruction on how to live, I can testify that it has been his lifelong obsession for near on 30 years. As that obsession has grown and matured, from my perspective, so has his confidence in the perfect provision available to any of us with eyes to see, ears to hear, and a heart to follow.

That confidence has borne fruit in his life in many ways; in timely and often miraculous provision for his practical needs, the stories of which, over the years, I can't even begin to count; in multiplying his witness of Christ as seeds planted in the hearts of anyone that comes across his path, be they a CEO of a large company or the pool cleaner visiting his home; and, perhaps most deeply, in an almost-unwavering trust in the goodness of God in both the lean times and the abundant ones.

Indeed, if Michael worries about anything, I have yet to see it. And he has never been one to play small, either, which comes with more than its fair share of opportunities to give in to anxiety. Instead, when the impulse comes, he leans into the abundant evidence of God's perfect provision expressed in this book; trusting daily provision like the hummingbird, waiting with confidence like the emperor penguin for food that always arrives at the perfect moment year after year, or riding the invisible currents of support like the eagle.

I have this unique vantage point because I am his son. And I asked to write this foreword so I could implore you to listen carefully to what he has to share in this extraordinary work. Because I know, firsthand, that it will, if applied, change your life.

Don't just treat this book as a way to scratch your intellectual curiosity. There are many wonderful books that will do that for you. Instead, treat it as a practical guide, a living map traced along the lines of God's perfect design, to follow into in the richness of God's worry-free abundance.

To Your Abundant Provision,

Ryan Pink

CONTENTS

FREED FROM PRISON

(Not Your Typical Introduction)

We were all born in prison. Slaves to sin. And we didn't know it. And because that's all we've ever known, we adapted our lives to that condition.

But it wasn't always that way. In the garden of Eden, at the beginning, we had no fear, no shame, no scarcity anxiety, no fear of lack, no oppressive toil, no separation from God. We had freedom and we had dominion.[1] And it was beautiful.

But the unthinkable happened in that garden through deception, and we were sold to sin.[2] No longer free, anxious toil became the norm. Fear and worry became our daily companions.

And from that day to this something inside us longs to regain that freedom, for that connection to God as our Father[3], to be delivered from anxious toil that drives us on, and from "the bondage of corruption into the glorious freedom of the children of God."[4]

Have we forgotten or did we not know that Jesus came to "proclaim liberty to the captives… to set at liberty those who are oppressed."[5] That it was for freedom that Christ has set us free[6]. We love to quote those verses, but so few experience the promise they contain.

Every man, and every woman, craves, and longs to be free. But yet, so many are shackled by the cares of this world, or the lust for other things entering and choking[7] and strangling and draining the life out of them. Keeping them from experiencing the promise they know is true, but have yet to experience. So they take a raincheck on the promise and settle for getting it in Heaven when they die.

But we are free right now. He has opened the prison doors. We are free to walk out and step into liberty, to be ***free as a bird***. Sadly, for most, they prefer the confines they've gotten used to... those long hours, and lost connection, not only with God, but even with their own family sharing the same prison cell with them. The door is open, but they prefer the familiar, and the consolation of their fellow inmates, as they sing songs about the sweet by and by, while the exhilaration of the amazing "here and now" passes by their window.

Heaven can wait. We have work to do on this earth[8], and that work is not burdensome, nor is it anxious toil. It is our destiny. We have a life of adventure and conquest and purpose awaiting our agreement to take hold of it – fearlessly, confidently, and faithfully. But will we? Will you?

When Jesus said, "Consider the birds"[9], He was addressing the universal condition of worry, which is a manifestation of fear. And He knew we were all slaves to fear[10]. So, He pointed out the birds.

They don't plant crops – God made sure their provision was planted for them.

They don't slave in the hot sun to gather up a barn full of supply, because they know it will never run out.

The world is their barn – no need to build one.

He used birds to deliver His message because they're everywhere. And they have this epic sense of freedom. We instinctively know it. We see them flying in the sky and wish we could that. We see some of them diving for fish and wish we could go fishing instead of grinding away at the office. We hear them singing in the morning their own song of freedom, and something within us, longs for that.

We want to be free from worry, from anxiety, from lack, and from burdensome debts. We've all carried the weight of learned behaviors and false beliefs that we didn't choose that enslave us, but they were ingrained into us when we were too young to know differently.

We were told this is the way life works. This is the way it will always be. But it doesn't have to be that way.

FREEDOM...

That is the cry of our heart, the cry of our soul. To be free... Free to make choices. Free to go where we want, when we want, in alignment with the high calling of God on our life[11]. Freedom to live a life full of joy and happiness, to live worry-free, never again concerned about provision.

This book is about true freedom, and how to find it. The freedom that every bird flying in the sky knows, that every eagle soaring above, every hummingbird flying across the Gulf of America, knows and lives. It is not freedom from work, but finding joy in the work He created you for, and in the process, having all your needs met according to His riches in glory by Christ Jesus[12].

In this book you will learn the keys to freedom. Not the kind of freedom the world promises that holds you captive to the lust and desires of your flesh, but the kind of freedom that frees your soul and opens up a world of possibilities that have eluded your notice before.

The freedom that beckons you to spend your life in a worthy cause, daring greatly, knowing that if you fail, you at least failed while daring greatly[13], not settling to be numbered among those timid souls too afraid to step out of the prison Christ freed them from.

In these pages, you will learn:

- How to craft the environment that shapes your future

- More than a dozen strategies to find the provision God has laid up for you
- Seven habits for gaining elevation in your business and life
- How and what to shed that no longer serves you
- How to tap into Heaven's compass to clarify God's direction for your life

I've written dozens of books, selling hundreds of thousands of copies. For forty years, I've been teaching Biblical strategies and natural laws for success in sales and business, leading sales turnarounds that include taking a struggling sales team of three, and helping it become the 16th fastest growing company in America on the INC 500 list. But in all my years, I've never had any revelation so transformative as this.

You're going to want to read and reread this book. It will change your life. I have been personally transformed in the writing of this book and I believe you will be transformed in the application of its truths. Be watching for our full training course and our 3-day transformation retreats to be held in amazing locations – coming soon!

"If the Son makes you free, you will be free indeed."[14]

Now turn the page to read the unusual origin story of how this book came to be that began with a miracle in the sky...

References: 1) Genesis 1:28 2) Romans 7:14 3) Romans 8:15. 4) Romans 8:21 5) Luke 4:18 6) Galatians 5:1 7) Mark 4:19 8) Ephesians 2:10 9) Luke 12:24 10) Hebrews 2:15 11) Philippians 3:14 12) Philippians 4:19 13) Teddy Roosevelt 14) John 8:36

THE ORIGIN STORY

"In all your ways acknowledge Him, and He shall direct your paths."[1]

It was a cool Florida evening during a much-anticipated Alabama–Tennessee showdown in Tuscaloosa which Alabama won (Roll Tide!) when a quiet stirring began to rise in my spirit. Judy and I enjoyed the game on TV, but beneath the surface, something deeper was awakening. At halftime, unwilling to ignore it, I stepped outside into the night. The hour was late, yet the stars were alive and shimmering – old friends sparkling against a dark velvet sky.

The heavens always fill me with wonder, but that night, every created thing seemed to hum with a deeper invitation. As I walked, a deep longing filled my heart. I told God plainly that I wanted to know Him more intimately than I know my wife… more truly than I know myself.

Then, beneath a moonless, crystal-clear sky, I asked Him directly if such longing was acceptable to Him. And at that very moment – something I could never have prepared for – the night sky flashed.

Twice.

No clouds. No distant storms. No earthly explanation. Just two sudden bursts of light across an otherwise silent heaven. Startled, humbled, almost afraid to hope, I whispered, "I'll take that as a 'yes.'" My next thought was almost childlike: "How will this unfold? Are You coming to my house… or am I going to Yours?" But the weeks that followed revealed a path I never imagined.

God began unveiling mysteries hidden in birds – mysteries tied to Matthew 6, where Jesus pointed to these fragile, feathered creatures and said, "Do not worry… your Father feeds them."

As I studied their God-woven wisdom, I realized I had stumbled onto a revelation that demanded to be captured, shared, and stewarded. Then Romans 1:20 illuminated the moment:

> "For since the creation of the world His invisible attributes – his eternal power and divine nature - are clearly seen, ***being understood by the things that are made...***"

I had asked to know Him more deeply, and He answered – by revealing facets of His eternal power and divine nature through the birds He fashioned with His own imagination. It was an unexpected visitation disguised as everyday creation. And so, I echo Paul's exultation:

> "Oh, the depth of the riches of the wisdom and knowledge of God! How unsearchable are His judgments, and His ways past finding out! For from Him and through Him and to Him are all things. To Him be the glory forever. Amen."[2]

The discovery itself began to unfold one morning as my Labradoodle, Judah, and I set out for our walk. The air was still cool, the light new, and the trees alive with unseen singers. As I passed beneath the oak branches draped in Spanish moss, I wondered what all the commotion was about. It felt celebratory, as though their team had just scored the go-ahead touchdown in the fourth quarter of a playoff game.

Walking past the lake, its glassy surface searching for the dawn's early light, I noticed, along its rocky but shallow shore, a heron standing like a statue, waiting for an unsuspecting fish to come within striking range.

Judah, fascinated by this tall, motionless creature, was a little suspicious of the heron and decided to investigate. After all, he feels it's his job to provide security for the neighborhood when he's out on patrol and, as he explained to me later, thought the heron was up to no good. As he approached the scraggly-looking heron, its cover now blown, it let out an angry squawk, muttering something derogatory about dogs as it headed off to the distant shore.

Continuing our walk, we came across two large red-headed sandhill cranes facing off against each other, doing the most ridiculous-looking dance ritual. They didn't take too kindly when Judah, with tail wagging, decided to introduce himself and offer to settle any dispute. Watching on the sidelines were a few great white egrets, slender and silent, with their golden beaks that look like bling, observing it all from a distance and keeping a wary eye on Judah. It was just another day in the bird sanctuary we call home.

In some ways, it's like an endless parade of spectacular birds, beautiful and diverse, that stop by the lake to see if the fish have repopulated and to visit relatives. On rare days, we are treated to the Roseate Spoonbill, a pink bird with a platypus-styled bill that glides across the water, surveying any number of the thirty-four species of ducks found in Florida, looking for that perfect place to wade and grab a bite to eat.

Have you ever paused to consider how the approximately 8.7 million different species on earth exist in intricate interdependence? The theory of chance evolution collapses in the light of any honest inquiry. Out of that innumerable and unbelievable diversity, there are just over 11,000 known bird species.

Before God created man in His image, He created birds and spoke directly to them[3], blessing them and instructing them to multiply on the earth. They've been doing that ever since, and according to Bird Life International, there are now some 50 billion individual wild birds globally.

And God feeds every one of them – daily. How's that for a responsibility?!

If God feeds 50 billion birds every day, do you really think it's a stretch for Him to come through for you?

What if I told you that God has already provided everything you will ever need for life and attached it to your purpose? And that...

Your anxious struggle for provision is misspent energy.
Your worry is nothing more than allegiance to the
kingdom of fear. Your fear repels provision.

What if I also told you that God fashioned your heart individually, uniquely, and purposefully? That you weren't mass-produced or the result of random selection? There is nothing generic about you. Psalm 33:15 clearly says that God, "fashioned your heart individually," and the Hebrew word for "fashioned" is *yatsar*, which implies blueprint-level intentionality. It suggests that He shaped your heart (your inner being) like a craftsman shaping clay, with His hands guiding and shaping the outcome with the love and vision He has for your life.

The inner architecture of your heart was shaped and personally tailored by God for a reason, a purpose, an assignment, that includes, indeed is fueled by deep connection with the Father and His Son, Jesus Christ. That is why Jesus instructed us to seek God's kingdom first and His righteousness[4], that we may know Him and learn from Him. In the process, everything we need in life, including our food, drink, and clothing, will be "added to us, laid beside us, annexed for us, and given to us" (MQP-AMP).

In Matthew 6:26, Jesus is offering us the birds as a form of instructive input. When you observe a hummingbird, for example, the world's smallest bird, draining nectar reserves from an exotic flower while hovering in place, with its wings beating five to ten times faster per second than a helicopter's rotor blade at full speed, it looks impossibly easy and wondrous at the same time.

As its microscopic feathers shimmer in the light, it dazzles not only with beauty but also in its stunning maneuverability, capable of flying forwards or backwards, even upside down, while its heart races at a stunning 1260 times per minute. Think of the sheer genius it took to pack all those capabilities and beauty into a creature that weighs less than a penny.

The hummingbird must consume roughly half its body weight in sugar daily, and may spend eight to twelve hours pursuing those calories, because its body runs on the edge of energetic impossibility, maintaining one of the highest metabolic rates in the bird world. If God can take such care in the design and feeding of the hummingbird, do you really think it's rational to be anxious about your own provision?

Jesus said,

> "Are not two sparrows sold for a copper coin? And not one of them falls to the ground apart from your Father's knowing and caring. Do not fear, therefore; you are of more value than many sparrows."[5]

The sparrow was considered virtually worthless due to its abundance, plain appearance, and small stature. Yet Jesus points out His Father's care for the seemingly insignificant and unremarkable little sparrow to make the point that if God cares for that little creature, won't He much more care for us who are made in His image and likeness?

Many of us live as though God's provision were uncertain, as if His care for us fluctuated with our performance. But Scripture instructs us otherwise:

> "Can a mother forget her nursing child? … Yet I will not forget you"[6].

And we know from Hebrews 6:18 that it is impossible for God to lie. So the issue is never one of God's neglect. I believe the issue is that we fail to see the provision He has laid up for us. Lack, at its root, is a spiritual / perception problem, not an unalterable physical reality.

Science tells us the human eye sees less than 0.0035 percent of the electromagnetic spectrum. That means most of reality is invisible to us. Let that sink in. Faith is the spiritual equivalent of a broader lens, enabling you to see what all along has been there but outside your range of vision. Paul called it "the eyes of your understanding"[7].

In reality...

Faith lets you see invisible abundance
before it becomes visible supply.

That's because God's provision often exists in realms our natural eyes cannot see. Not to sound mystical here, but the reality is that often the solution to our needs is just one inspired idea away.

Think of faith as the lens through which we can see the invisible, those things that have not yet been created but could be, and are waiting for both your discovery and activation by faith. It interprets what the physical eye cannot: unseen realities that are eternal[8] and therefore superior to the temporary circumstances around us.

Everything in creation moves from the unseen realm to the seen. Thought precedes form. In Genesis 1, over and over again, God spoke what He saw, and it was so. First the unformed image, then the physical reality.

Before there is manifestation,
there is always imagination.

Everything man has ever designed and built was first seen in the realm of imagination.

Faith acts on the unseen realm before the evidence to support that idea necessarily appears. Faith doesn't wait for the visible to form before it speaks; it defines reality and then it forms.

> "By faith we understand that the worlds were framed by the word of God, so that the things which are seen were not made of things which are visible"[9].

When Jesus told us to behold the birds, He wasn't virtue signaling. He was revealing the functional operating system of the kingdom. So it is with God's provision. We are invited to rule not by striving in the visible, but by contending earnestly for the faith[10] and boldly acting from what we see in the unseen realm and bringing it into the visible.

Walk outside early and watch the birds. Observe their habits and drink in their joy. They're not anxious about provision. They seem to know they will be fed. Does God drop food into their nests? No. They instinctively abide by habits encoded into their DNA – habits we can learn, apply, and prosper by.

This book is a journey through those habits, which include things like: flow with your design, forage daily, and shape your environment. Each one reveals a law of provision hidden in plain sight. If you want to know how to enter the life of worry-free provision, keep reading.

In Chapter 1, you will see what Jesus meant when He told us to stop worrying about provision and invited us to learn from the wisdom He instilled in birds. Let the birds teach you.

Now, turn the page… □

References: 1) Proverbs 3:6 2) Romans 11:33, 36 3) Genesis 1:22 4) Matthew 6:33 5) Matthew 10:29–31 6) Isaiah 49:15 7) Ephesians 1:18 8) 2 Corinthians 4:18 9) Hebrews 11:3 10) Jude 1:3

CHAPTER 1

GOD'S WINGED MESSENGERS OF WISDOM

Learning From The Birds

"But now ask the beasts, and they will teach you; and the birds of the air, and they will tell you." (Job 12:7)

If birds could testify, you would never again doubt God's faithfulness. Every bird on earth is well taken care of by God, but perhaps one of the more amazing examples of trust and provision is the Emperor Penguin from the land of Antarctica, because its whole life depends on provision arriving *exactly* when needed. No room for error.

It all begins in the heart of winter, when the female lays a single egg, and then carefully positions it on the top of her hubby's feet. He stands there like many new fathers, with an awkward look on his face, as if to say, "Now what?!?" He's hesitant to move, in case he drops it on the ice, and it rolls into the ocean. He feels a bit stuck, really. He has no hands to reposition the egg. All he can really do is stand there, or shuffle very slowly near other new father penguins for warmth.

Meanwhile, momma penguin dawdles off to the coast to go fishing and get food. He has no choice but to pretty much stand in one place, despite 100 mph winds and temperatures 60 degrees below zero, and cover the egg under a fold of warm brood skin. For over two months, he doesn't go anywhere. He doesn't eat or drink. Weeks pass. Darkness swallows him. The sun has vanished completely, with no promise of return. Snow blankets him while the wind howls, but he never doubts. He waits.

Then it happens: the shell cracks open, and the most adorable but helpless little chick emerges. So cute, and so hungry. But the daddy penguin planned for this. He had been saving one last meal the whole time, a curd-like solution in his throat, which he gives to his chick. Thing is, he has no more he can feed the chick after that, and if momma doesn't come back soon, both will perish.

Not to worry. Somehow, she knows it's time, and navigates hundreds of miles in shifting sea ice, returning to the exact colony she left months earlier. The father still cannot see her. The chick cannot call to her, and there are no landmarks in this barren, treeless world of white. Yet she finds him by recognizing his voice, and brings back a partially digested belly full of fish to feed the chick.

The timing is razor thin. If she was a few days late, both the chick and the father would likely die. But that doesn't happen. Instead, generation after generation, the pattern holds. Despite there being no sowing or reaping or barns to store provision, they confidently wait with full expectation. This story repeats every year with every penguin pair. The miracle of provision is not considered exceptional. It's how God designed it to work, and they just cooperate with their design, trusting the timing and experiencing His faithfulness.

It took too many years for me to understand that God essentially wrote two books: the book of His Word (the Bible), and the book of His works, which we call creation, or the created order. As rich as the Bible is, it in no way is the sum total of God's knowledge or revelation to man. Even John the Apostle said,

> "And there are also many other things that Jesus did, which if they were written one by one, I suppose that even the world itself could not contain the books that would be written."[1]

The Apostle Paul reminds us that we can learn about God by the things that are made[2], and it was Solomon who taught wisdom from the book of God's creation. In 1 Kings 4, it says that he...

> "Spoke of trees, from the cedar tree of Lebanon even to the hyssop that springs out of the wall; he spoke also of animals, **OF BIRDS**, of creeping things, and of fish. And men of all nations, ***from all the kings of the earth*** who had heard of his wisdom, came to hear the wisdom of Solomon."

Did you know that Solomon spoke about birds? I didn't. It stands to reason, that if he spoke of them, he must have studied them. What did he learn and what did he teach that attracted the attention of kings? Hopefully this book taps into some of that. Then, in the fullness of time, Jesus came, and in His famous Sermon on the Mount, said...

> "Do not WORRY about your life, what you will eat or what you will drink; nor about your body, what you will put on. Is not life more than food and the body more than clothing? BEHOLD the fowls of the air, for they neither sow nor reap nor gather into barns; yet your heavenly Father feeds them. Are you not of more value than they?"[3]

"Behold" in Greek (*katanoeō*) means to perceive deeply, to study attentively. Jesus could have said "look at the birds" as some sort of passing comment, but He said "*Behold*", which, in a very literal sense, means to "hold them with your eyes." The idea being to study them until we understand.

In Luke 12:24, Jesus says,

> "Consider the ravens, for they neither sow nor reap, which have neither storehouse nor barn; and God feeds them. Of how much more value are you than the birds?"

"Consider" in Greek (*emblépō*) means "to look into," or "to gaze intently upon." It's the idea of fixing your eyes on something with intentional, purposeful focus to gain revelation. Either word requires us to look deeper into the wisdom of God embedded in the beauty and mystery of birds, if we want to know how to live free as a bird with nothing lacking, nothing broken, and nothing missing, never again concerned about provision.

I walk my dog every morning. Sometimes, if I go early enough, when the air is still cool and the light only beginning to spill over the horizon, I will be treated to a concert of birds overhead, crowding every tree limb, singing, and chattering with a sound that carries your soul to the heavens, if you let it.

Sometimes, to add a bit of drama to the performance, something will spark them en masse to take flight to destinations unknown. It's then that I understand what David said in Psalm 19:1...

> "The heavens declare the glory of God, and the sky displays (proclaims - ESV) what His hands have made."

On those days, the sky is alive with His handiwork on full display. He invites all of us to look closer as the sky fills with the wonder of God. David went on to say that...

> "Their sound has gone out into the entire world, their message to the ends of the earth."[4]

If Job said that birds will tell you something, and David confirmed the sky proclaims a message for all the earth, and his son Solomon amazed the leaders of his day by sharing wisdom he had gleaned from birds, among other things, and if Jesus (a greater One than Solomon) directly admonished us to behold the birds, maybe we should do that. Job, David, and Solomon were in some way instructed by observing the wisdom of God on display in birds. Coincidentally, they were also some of the wealthiest men of antiquity.

I'm not saying that learning the secrets God embedded in birds will make you wealthy, but Jesus did promise we would never have to worry about provision again if we learned how to tap into the flow of God's abundance like birds do every day. That feels pretty flush to me.

I'm blown away by the simple faith of a hummingbird that can fly 500 miles nonstop across the Gulf of America to a place it has never seen, fueled by faith in the provision of flowers it hasn't yet found, and knows it will be nourished and replenished upon its arrival.

The level of detailed engineering, and pure wisdom built into a hummingbird, though impressive, pales in comparison to what God built into you. If God put that much attention and detail into a bird that may only live 3 to 5 years and makes sure that every one of them never lacks for provision, does it make any sense to you that He may have overlooked His own children?

Every book I've written first came to me as an idea. I saw it in my mind's eye. Then I went to work on it. That one simple truth has resulted in hundreds of thousands of books sold. All of it by faith in an idea that took on form and became provision.

Faith acts on what is true before the physical evidence of that truth appears. Faith doesn't deny reality. It sculpts it.

> "By faith we understand that the worlds were framed by the word of God, so that the things which are seen were not made of things which are visible."[5]

Our problem is never the lack of provision. God has no shortages. Ever. We simply don't perceive the provision He has provided because it often comes in the form of a problem that needs solving. Every problem that comes your way has an equal or greater opportunity attached to it. Once you understand that, everything changes.

Think of problems as though they were some type of nut. Every nut is protected by a shell. Break open the shell, you get the provision. Simple. The bigger the nut, the greater the provision. Some problems are the size of a peanut. Others are the size of a coconut. Instead of going into the fetal position when a big problem comes your way, rejoice, knowing that it carries with it a big reward. You will never find an unopened nutshell that doesn't have a nut inside.

The bigger the problem, the bigger the opportunity!
Birds demonstrate that reality in many different ways. For example, strong winds create powerful updrafts, giving lift to birds, making flight almost effortless. Stormy weather is generally regarded as a negative thing, but albatrosses fly into roaring ocean winds, extracting energy from wind shear. Likewise, eagles and hawks gain altitude from the storm and rise above it.

> What looks like resistance is often just
> stored energy waiting to be harnessed.

The hummingbird's metabolism is through the roof, requiring tremendous energy to maintain. Their ninja-like flying skills enable them to access nectar sources most others cannot. That allows them to feed (and pollinate) where competition is scarce. The niche they occupy is only accessible to creatures with extreme abilities. God made it so the bird with the highest energy demand could find and access the richest source of supply.

Look at the Bar-headed Goose… These birds take their flying seriously! They migrate over the Himalayas (the highest mountain range in the world), where the oxygen is thin, the temperatures sub-zero, and the winds are cruel and unrelenting. They're designed with more efficient lungs, unbelievable endurance, and their bodies optimize oxygen more easily and more effectively for those high-altitude flights.

The environment doesn't defeat the goose; it helps define it! Birds don't improve by avoiding difficulty. They improve by learning how to fly inside the difficulty. What looks like opposition is often compressed provision waiting to be discovered. It reminds me of when Joseph, who had been sold into slavery and rose to be second only to the Pharaoh of Egypt, said to his brothers who betrayed him…

> "But as for you, you meant evil against me; but God meant it for good, in order to bring it about as it is this day, to save many people alive."[6]

Those who live by that perspective tend to see stronger wind as greater lift, longer distances as larger territory, and bigger threats as a means to develop smarter systems. The harder the battle, the greater the prize.

For example, when the twelve spies returned from checking out the Promised Land, ten of them gave a negative report about the size of the giants. But Joshua and Caleb said those giants were their very provision, and they were well able to take the land. They saw the problem as their provision[7]!

James said to ...

> "Count it all joy when you fall into various trials, knowing that the testing of your faith produces patience. But let patience have its perfect work, that you may be perfect and complete, lacking nothing."[8]

If you're facing a big problem right now, rejoice because there is always a really big opportunity with it, designed to make sure you lack nothing. The opportunity may not be readily obvious, but Psalm 34:10 says...

> "The young lions lack and suffer hunger; But those who seek the Lord shall not lack any good thing."

From my perspective, that means it's incumbent upon us to seek the Lord and ask Him to show us the opportunity, along with the wisdom and instruction to turn that opportunity into provision. Maybe that provision is financial. It often is. But maybe it's an insight or word of wisdom that turns the tide in a difficult situation or negotiation. But when we follow through on what He shows us when we seek Him, we will not lack any good thing. Easier said than done, but I speak from proven experience forged in the fires of existential threats to my business.

So it doesn't come across as mystical, let me put it in practical terms with an example… In my second printing of *The Bible Incorporated*, I ordered another 25,000 leather-bound copies. The only way I could pay for them was to presell thousands of copies.

For this print run, I had taken care of that with a major ministry pre-ordering 5,000 customized copies as part of the larger print run. Because they were customized with their name and logo, they had to prepay. They kept delaying payment, but finally, on the day the presses were about to start printing, they canceled their order.

Without their order and prepayment, I had no way to pay the bill. It was devastating news. If I couldn't pay, I couldn't print. If I couldn't print, I didn't have a business. If I didn't have a business, what was I going to do? That was a supersized coconut problem for me!

I called my wife and told her of this serious problem and asked her to come to the office so we could pray that God would reveal the opportunity that I knew must be there, but was currently not visible to me. By the time she arrived, I had already heard from the Lord. We still ordered 25,000 copies, but only 5,000 would be leather-bound. The rest were paperbacks. The paperback version was so popular that it far outsold the leather version and became our bestselling book ever!

Maybe your problem is not financial in nature, and you're wondering how there could be an opportunity attached to it that dwarfs the magnitude of the problem. That is a valid question, and I will speak from my direct experience…

In May of 1978, Jennifer Lynn, my first-born child, came into the world. I remember two things that were on my mind in the days leading up to her birth. I was hoping my child would have ten toes and ten fingers, which she did. But there was something else lurking in my soul… a fear… so real I never spoke of it. After all, there was no justification for such a fear.

That fear was that I would have a Down Syndrome child. The fear of having a child with that condition gnawed on my soul like a rat gnawing on a bone. It turned out that, like Job[9], the thing I feared greatly came upon me.

The next morning, however, I rose early, wrapped her in a blanket, and laid her gently cooing body on the living room carpet. As I was beguiled by her innocence, it dawned on me that God's love for us is not conditional upon our perfection or lack thereof. If God loves us unconditionally, how could I not extend unconditional love to my baby?

I came to terms that morning with the reality that she would never have a normal life, never go to school, get married, have kids of her own, etc. She would need special care and attention her entire life. I realized that the challenges before me could either make me bitter or better. I chose the latter.

I told my wife that because of her condition, we had the opportunity to gain wisdom way beyond our years. I said that all our friends at church got stuck with normal kids, but we had an opportunity that not many people have, and we could grow wise and deep and have a rich life.

As the months went by and the permanency of her condition sank in, I asked God how to think of it. Lying in bed that night, He directed me to 2 Corinthians 4:17, which reads,

> "For our light affliction, which is but for a moment, is working for us a far more exceeding and eternal weight of glory."

Wow! What a promise! What a perspective! An "exceeding and eternal weight of glory"?! How was I so fortunate to have this happen? I was overjoyed with His promise, and I realized my choice from day one to see this as an opportunity for profound growth was not a denial of reality, but rather an embracing of eternal truth.

For eighteen months our inner capacity grew, and wisdom became our portion. I had no idea that you could love so deeply and be loved back in the way she did. While others pitied us, we were living a quiet life of daily joy. Her handicap was our hand up in life.

But then, six days before Christmas in 1979, after having open-heart surgery the previous month to correct a leaking valve, she died on the day we were to bring her home. I had never been to a funeral. Now I was planning my daughter's.

The child I had bonded to stronger than super glue was suddenly and unexpectedly gone. The Christmas presents I had bought for her would never be opened. Her toys at home, meant to bring joy to her, only brought tears to our eyes. Where was the glimmer of light now? How could something good proceed out of that? Sure, she was in heaven playing with angels, but my heart, it seemed, was buried with her.

At the cemetery, a friend approached with what he believed to be a message from God for us. He said that God would multiply the fruit of my wife's womb. Somehow that felt like much more than a hopeful sentiment from a friend. It felt like it came directly from the throne of God. It was so real to us that we were filled once again with joy and were trying to hide our laughter as we drove out of the cemetery.

Sure enough, nine months later, my wife gave birth to another daughter, Amy Joy, AND her fraternal twin, Ryan. The fruit of her womb was indeed multiplied! I don't pretend to have life all figured out. It can be very hard at times, but God will, with that trial, give us what we need, to get through[10] so we can come out better and stronger, even more joyful. I believe God loves us more than we will ever live long enough to fully grasp. He gave up His Son for us to die naked on a cross after being brutally whipped with His flesh torn apart. What is our trial compared to that?

I have put my own depth meter into the love of God and found it immeasurable. The deeper I go, the deeper I understand it to be. The more you know how much God loves you, the more you realize how little you really know the depth and full measure of that love, because His love is truly measureless.

If your life has had tragedy in it, don't blame God. Jesus said that in this world you will have tribulation, but be of good cheer, because He has overcome the world! You may not feel that cheer at the moment. That I understand. Psalm 30:5 says that "weeping may endure for a night, but joy comes in the morning." We can turn it down, delay it, or receive it. The sooner we're able to receive it, the sooner our healing comes, and the stronger we become, which makes us able to help others and be an agent, even a dispenser, of God's love.

Near where I live, there is an eagle's nest. On occasion I will see that eagle circling on high, riding invisible columns of air, trusting the wind to do the heavy lifting. I never see it frantically flapping its wings… It simply glides on harnessed, unseen energy.

How often in our lives have we tried to manufacture lift by effort alone? Birds teach us many things, but perhaps the most poignant is learning to align with invisible forces, columns of faith, timing, and grace, and let those carry us to heights we never imagined, and that raw energy never could.

As I began to follow the directive from Jesus to "consider the ravens" and "behold the fowls," I got curious. Real curious. What else might I find of God's wisdom built into the design and function of every bird in the over 11,000 species He feeds daily? They neither fret nor hoard, yet they're fed. God doesn't drop food in their nests. They're creatures of habit, with constant access to unlimited provision.

Provision is so abundant that they never have to store it up in an extra nest someplace. They know where and how to get what they need when they need it. And they never have to worry about it.

If you want to live free as a bird, accessing God's unlimited provision, it begins with Chapter 2…

Flow With Your Design – How Design Reveals Purpose

References: 1) John 21:25 2) Romans 1:20 3) Matthew 6:25-26 4) Psalm 19:4 5) Hebrews 11:3 6) Genesis 50:20 7) Numbers 14:9 8) James 1:2-4 9) Job 3:25 10) 1 Corinthians 10:13

CHAPTER 2

FLOW WITH YOUR DESIGN

Design Reveals Purpose

"Design is destiny in seed form"

I just got back from walking Judah. The weather is perfect for a December morning – sunny, seventy degrees, the slightest hint of a breeze, and the scent of distant citrus flowers wafting in the air.

The lake was slightly ruffled by the breeze and was entertaining a flock of dozens of cormorants swimming in formation across the water. Every once in a while, most of them would suddenly dive underwater as a school of small fish passed by. Watching from just behind was a pelican, letting the cormorants locate and signal where the fish were, and then swooping in to catch what he could.

Their unique fishing habits were both strategic and entertaining. On the shoreline, a great white egret, a little blue heron, and a great blue heron seemed slightly annoyed by all the disturbance not far from shore. After all, they don't chase fish… They're too smart for that… They wait for the fish to come to them! Apparently, so does the alligator I passed, who, upon detecting our presence, made a big splash and submerged all but his bulging eyeballs as he stared back in utter contempt.

What's striking about this scene, is that none of them chose their role in the fishing derby unfolding before me. They didn't audition for their part. They simply cooperate with their God-given design because they were made for it.

Earlier this morning, before the sun rose from its chamber, it gave off the slightest silver edge of light, tickling the treetops and gently waking its inhabitants. As the night dissolved and shadows retreated, the lake which would soon attract the eagles and osprey was throwing off what little heat it had left from warmer days, forming a wispy layer of morning fog that clung to the water in a vain attempt to shield the fish below.

In the sacredness of the silence, a bird cleared its throat and, in an unhurried and impossibly confident tone, proceeded to give his rendition of reveille. In mere moments, other birds resting in the branches began to join in. The mourning dove waited a few minutes and then treated the world to a sound only a dove can make, and with that sound brought a calming peace.

Every facet of creation is inscribed with purpose by God Himself. He thought… then He spoke, and the form appeared. Not as some random lump of clay, but as an innumerable host of creatures intricately dependent on each other, revealing elegant designs, beautiful forms, and purposeful functions that we are still discovering.

Nothing God crafted was incidental. Every bone, feather, wing, sinew – even their mental capacity and built-in instincts, carried the imprint of God's intentionality. As the psalmist said in Psalm 19:1...

> "The heavens declare the glory of God; the skies proclaim the work of His hands."

And in doing so, the birds showcase His wisdom.

Birds don't question their design or struggle to find their purpose. They don't try to overwrite their God-given design, nor do they strive to be something they're not. You'll never see a robin diving for fish or an osprey hunting for worms. You'll never see a sparrow trying to be an eagle or a crow trying to hover like a hummingbird.

The first secret of their success is that they flow with their design. They know instinctively that their design reveals purpose, and in cooperating with that design, they never lack for food. The woodpecker doesn't hide its chisel-like beak in embarrassment. The swan never apologizes for its regal elegance. The nightingale doesn't mute its voice in fear of what other, less-talented songbirds might think. All of creation reflects the wisdom of God, designed with exquisite precision, crafted for a life only it can live.

The birds are inscribed with a theology of purpose, which states that...

Design reveals purpose and
structure indicates assignment.

God never leaves His creation without a way not only to survive, but to thrive. What would happen if we treated our gifts, our unique attributes, even our deepest, innermost longings, not as suggestions, but as assignments? What if we saw our wiring as revelation, not inconvenience?

Get up before dawn and treat yourself to the grand awakening, where light, like transparent gold fills the sky and chases shadows from east to west. And as the sky fills with birds on their daily mission, remember that...

Design is destiny in seed form.

Purpose is hardcoded into you before you even know it's there. When we embrace what God made us to be, we become what we were always meant to be.

Every day you can see the birds rise into the sky, not by brute force, but by design; not by anxious striving, but by surrender to God and the design with which He crafted them; not by imitation of something else, but by the identity they were given. That's a lesson for us... Don't let the world tell you who you are. Don't let anyone else define you.

Think of it: God clothed the lily more spectacularly than royalty. He feeds the lowly sparrow, and 50 billion other birds daily. But to us, who are created in His image and likeness, we are equipped with precise, Spirit-crafted capacity for the work He prepared before time began. We have purpose and mission and destiny, and we have everything we need to fulfill it.

There is no question as to whether God designed you with intention. He did. The question is whether you will live in alignment with it.

When Jesus instructed us to "behold the fowls of the air" or to "consider the ravens," He wasn't using poetic jargon to give us fleeting inspiration. He was pointing us to a living model of economics that demonstrates the invisible laws of provision, so we never need worry about that again.

Birds live by design, not by demand. They don't wake up feeling the pressure of expectation from others. They wake up at peace with what they were designed to do. They don't live in constant response to pressure. They live in response to purpose, a purpose revealed in their design. Birds don't try to meet demands that violate their design.

Demand creates stress. Design taps into flow. Demand always pushes you to do more, do it faster, do it right now. Design says, "Do what you were made for, at the right time and in the right way." Life is better that way!

Birds operate in this world by what they are. They don't wake up one morning and decide what they're going to be. They don't choose to identify as a pigeon when they're really a chickadee. They simply obey what they already are. That's what it means to live by design.

Demands come in the form of genuine external pressures such as localized scarcity, bad weather, predators, and competition. But birds don't restructure their lives around anxiety by hoarding obsessively, working beyond their capacity, or abandoning their rhythms because "times are difficult." They respond from design, not from worry or fear. Demands shout at us, but design whispers. Listen to the whisper. Birds never step outside their nature to secure provision. Provision meets them as they conform and operate within their design. Birds do that by instinct, but for us, it's a choice.

Therefore, faith in its purest form is obedience to design.

When you live by design, you choose the work God prepared for you, not just more lifeless work. You move with a sense of inner timing, not a bullying urgency. When you are confident in your design and flowing with it, you trust that provision will show up instead of going into contortions and forcing outcomes. Birds don't chase someone else's opportunities. They are so aligned with their design that, in following the design, opportunities appear.

When you hold creation in the grip of your gaze, reflecting deeply on its design and purpose, and contemplating the wonder of its form and the wisdom of its function, a level of revelation unfolds. It's really the revealing of some of the attributes of God that He wants you to learn.

Have you ever seen a falcon in action? It's the embodiment of calibrated precision, divine purpose, and speed. The falcon is not just another bird. To watch one in flight is to witness a masterclass in design and functionality. It is so perfectly tuned to its purpose that every feather, every structure within its body, even its heartbeat, moves in perfect harmony with its calling.

There is nothing on earth any faster. A peregrine falcon can exceed speeds of 240 miles per hour in a dive, but that blinding speed is not chaos. It is controlled excellence, serenity at high speed, and alignment under gravity. It's made possible, in part, because of the built-in baffles in its nostrils that function like jet-engine regulators, keeping the air from tearing its lungs apart.

It's not just blindingly fast; it was designed for spectacular feats and engineered to handle greatness, gaining its incredible acceleration from its streamlined, teardrop body, stiff tapered wings, and cooperation with natural laws. If you will afford your mind the privilege of reasoned curiosity and borderless imagination, you'll discover the vastness of your own God-ordained potential that comes to life when purpose and preparation align, and speed comes with ease.

A falcon has its choice of prey, so it doesn't chase everything that moves across its path. It watches from a high altitude, able to spot a pigeon a mile away. It waits. When the math aligns with the physics, it commits body, mind, and focus to one target, rarely missing.

It demonstrates the secret power of
intense focus, unfettered by hesitation.

In similar fashion, when you decide, I mean truly decide, seemingly formidable circumstances will bend under the weight of your conviction, and you'll cut through resistance like a hot knife through butter, because that's what you were designed for.

In Ecclesiastes 9:11, Solomon identifies the importance of speed, but goes on to mention that as important as speed is, timing is even more important. That's why you can watch a falcon hover silently high in the sky, not moving, just suspended between heaven and earth.

You're not observing weakness or hesitation. You're looking at power held in reserve, waiting for that perfect moment, demonstrating that stillness precedes acceleration, and the greatest breakthroughs don't typically arise out of frantic motion, but rather from those quiet moments in heavenly places when you hear clearly, and your vision sharpens.

God invites us to live from our position seated with Christ in heavenly places[1] where we can see the larger picture, rise above the noise and traffic of the world, and strike only when the moment that has been prepared for us presents itself. You were not made to live life on a low level. You were made to ride the wind, get some lift, and gain perspective you simply can't get from the ground. From that elevated viewpoint, you can see clearly and strike with confidence and precision.

When you flow with your design, your life gains
an ease of grace you would otherwise miss out on.

Now perhaps you've read a motivational book or two but haven't experienced the success their seeds of greatness promised. You need look no further than the woodpecker, the drummer of the forest. The woodpecker stands out among forest creatures and seems to delight in all the attention. Adorned with a striking coat of black-and-white plumage and a perfectly coifed "hairdo" of vibrant red feathers on his head, he is the rock star of North American forest birds.

Then, as if to cement his reputation as a rock star, he bangs his head against solid wood all day long, striking the tree up to 20 times per second and delivering a force over 1,000 times greater than gravity! Yet because of his unique design, he suffers no brain damage.

Why? Because God gave the woodpecker a tongue so long that it wraps around the inside of his skull like a built-in safety harness protecting his brain from the constant jolts it receives when hammering against a tree.

It is so intricate and incredibly effective that engineers still study it today. And it's not just the tongue as a safety harness that protects him: his skull bones are spongy in front and dense in back to redirect impact. His beak is a tad longer on top than on the bottom, which helps disperse vibration forward instead of back into the brain.

Any other bird striking hardwood with its beak would quickly be destroyed if it repeated the blows, but for the woodpecker, every beat of his beak against the tree becomes a rhythm of purpose, a reminder of his unique advantage in the forest that no other creature can match. The woodpecker doesn't weaken under pressure… pressure becomes the tool that builds it. He's doing what he was made to do, and loves doing it!

That doesn't mean it's smooth sailing for the woodpecker. He doesn't simply go to a tree, knock politely on the trunk, and the insects come out for him to eat. Nope. He has to work for it, but that's okay, because he's also built for it. He may chip and chisel with his beak 8,000 to 12,000 times in a day. He doesn't give up when the bark is thick or when the opening he's created fills with sap, which it often does. He just keeps tapping on that tree like he's in a drum corps, tapping to the tempo of destiny while playing the soundtrack of "*Wipeout*" by the 1960's beach band, The Surfaris.

He seems to live by the motto, "I will persist until I succeed," made famous in Og Mandino's bestseller, *The Greatest Salesman in the World.* The woodpecker seems to know instinctively that if he keeps his rhythm, the breakthrough will come… because it always does.

The woodpecker's confidence about his place in the forest is steadfast and fearless. While most creatures look for a way to hide and not stand out, the woodpecker makes no bones about his presence, making it known with his unmistakable drumming sound that can be heard easily up to a half-mile away.

It's not arrogance on display. He's just staking his claim in the forest, marking out his territory, and hopefully attracting a mate who finds his drumming and work ethic irresistible. When you flow with your God-given design, your "sound" will stand out and attract those called to build with you. Just like the woodpecker, you weren't made to quietly fit in; you were made for distinction, and to release a sound that resonates with those you were meant to do life with. 1 Corinthians 14:8 says,

> "For if the trumpet makes an uncertain sound, who will prepare for battle?"

Stand out with recognizable distinction. Make your message clear. Be bold, so others can join you in the battle to take kingdom territory.

Like every other creature in the forest, the woodpecker's success is not a fluke of randomness or the result of evolution. It is by design. Every part of its anatomy, the shape of its skull, the length and placement of its tongue to cradle its brain, the shape of its beak, even its feet and tail, work together in perfect alignment with its purpose. And this is one of life's greatest secrets: when you flow with your design, your purpose becomes clear, your impact becomes legacy, and provision flows as a natural and endless byproduct.

The woodpecker is the perfect picture of James 2:26, demonstrating that faith without works is dead. It doesn't see the insects inside the wood before it begins. There was no message from God to go to a specific tree with an angel standing beside it. He just knows that if he does what he was designed to do, he will find success. He trusts that the reward he has not yet seen, will be revealed when he takes the right action. That is the message of faith:

Strike where purpose calls and where design allows,
and life will yield its hidden provision.

The next time you hear the forest drummer using his head as a jackhammer against the side of an oak tree, you're hearing more than the sound of drumming, you're hearing a message from God played out in rhythm. Beneath the beats of his beak, if you listen carefully, you'll hear God's message to you:

> "Don't quit because it's hard. Failure is not an option. Keep pressing on. Keep the faith. The treasure you seek has been laid aside for you. Do not grow weary in the good work you are doing, for in due season you will reap if you faint not."[2]

Truth is, every one of God's creatures is a teacher, not by words, but by their design, which they follow instinctively. It is in the following of their design, and not trying to be something else, that they don't suffer from lack, neither do they worry about finding provision. It's always there.

When you study them, you're learning something about the ways, wisdom, and wonder of God. Go beyond the superficial appearance and you will find modeled for you, keys for happy, successful, worry-free living. Their design and function reveal leadership keys, spiritual truths, even inalienable success principles that, if emulated, will bring a freedom you never knew was possible.

When I step outside my home, I find incredible beauty in unlikely, largely overlooked spaces. While many are looking for the grand gestures of God, magnificent mountain ranges or far-flung galaxies, I find beauty even in the grass and tiny flowers beneath my feet as I walk by the lake.

As I cast my glance skyward, usually at the shriek of a hawk or the calming call of a dove, I see wonders that others miss. Perhaps they're checking their email on the phone as they walk, or just absorbed in their own thoughts. But as for me, I want to know God deeply, and God's attributes and nature are knowable and on display in the things He created.[3]

While my neighbors may be otherwise engaged, I am utterly captivated as the horizon begins to blush just before the sun crests it. It creates a sense of awe and anticipation in me. On some days, a gentle breeze off the lake will arise, teasing my senses, drawing me into awareness, prepping me to notice the soon-to-be-playing orchestra of confidence, a choir of diverse voices, singing and chatting, inviting me to join in this chorus of praise to God and declare my own territorial boundaries that God has etched on my heart.

It's as if creation itself greets each day, all dressed up in light and music, eagerly anticipating what Paul referred to as the revealing of the sons of God[4]. While humanity carries on its path, creation seems to ask… Will it be today? Most people give creation a passing glance. Few behold it. But when you do, when you hold it with your eyes, you can begin to discern patterns and rhythms, how birds move according to an inner design that matches their outer design and purpose. They act on what has been inscribed in their nature. It feels totally natural for them to act the way they do.

While a hummingbird might think a woodpecker is crazy for knocking its head against a tree when there's such great nectar in virtually every flower, the woodpecker might think the hummingbird is crazy to flap its wings so furiously and even fly upside down when it can eat while parked on the side of a tree. There's no class envy in the forest. Every creature flows with its unique design, is fulfilled doing it, and can hardly wait for the next day when it can do it all over again.

When you flow with your design, it will never feel
like you're working another day in your life!

This is one of God's laws of provision: trust the design, and you will never want for provision again. Flowing in your design and working diligently in cooperation with it, is not a denial of faith in God's provision, it is the evidence of faith!

Consider the Bar-tailed Godwit? How's that for a name?! Every autumn, the godwits gather in Alaska for a family reunion and feasting, nearly doubling their body weight. Kind of like our Thanksgiving gatherings. But then, unlike us, they launch out over the Pacific Ocean and proceed to fly up to eleven days and nights nonstop, no potty breaks, no stopping for food or drink, traveling 7,000 to 8,000 miles to Australia and New Zealand, where they will spend their winters. God designed them with this capability, and they are a biological wonder of fuel efficiency and navigational skill.

As if that wasn't incredible enough, even the juvenile birds who have never attempted such a feat, will, in an unbelievable display of God's design for them, attempt their very first migration… alone… weeks after their parents have departed. What blows my mind is that somehow, they know where Australia and New Zealand are, and without a map, compass, or engine, they make a journey that seems utterly impossible to us. Clearly, God designed and equipped them for this amazing feat. That makes me want to explore more deeply how God designed us, and for what exploits!

And just for fun, let me introduce you to another marvel of God's creation. Weighing in at roughly three ounces, the Arctic tern makes the longest migration of any creature on Earth. Every year, they fly from their breeding grounds in the high Arctic all the way to the pack ice of Antarctica and back again, a trip of nearly 50,000 miles. Over the course of their lifetime, they will have flown the equivalent of three trips to the moon and back!

It's a journey into the unknown over an unpredictable expanse of ocean, with winds that occasionally blow them off course, without so much as a bag lunch. No map. No compass. No detailed itinerary. Even if they could use those things, they wouldn't, because for them, those tools are astonishingly inferior to the design functionality God built into them.

They come into this world with a genetically encoded "knowing" that somehow the sun, the stars, the earth's magnetic fields, and even the ocean currents will guide them to their needed sustenance along the way.

The Arctic tern doesn't worry; it simply navigates.

Birds come hardwired with a built-in knowing, part instinct and part intuition. There's no need to question the wiring… they just flow with the design God gave them. Pretty simple really. All-you-can-eat whenever you want to eat… and then ride the wind… all without bank loans, creditors, or financial worries.

Their key to survival and to enjoying a long, well-satiated life, is simply to do what they were made to do.

> The key to success in life lies in knowing how God fashioned your heart, discovering the work (mission) you were uniquely designed to fulfill[5], and discerning God's timing – when to start, when to migrate, when to stay and hold your ground[6].

Whether it's an osprey hovering motionless above the water, suspended between the tension in its wings and the variableness of the wind, or a barn swallow tracing an invisible design in the air with impossible aerobatics, all birds share the same sky, the same air, even the same God. But they have totally unique designs, and every one of them thrives and lives with joy, not by imitating each other, but by being true to their design.

Think about it: the robin cannot hover like a hummingbird. The hummingbird cannot soar like an eagle. The eagle cannot dive like a falcon. The falcon cannot migrate 7,000 miles like the bar-tailed godwit. And the beautiful thing is that God does not ask them to.

Birds, like people, thrive most when living in harmony with their God-given design, and tend to struggle more when trying to function outside of it.

Truth is, you were never meant to succeed
by being a copy of someone else.

You succeed by flowing with the unique, hand-crafted design you were given, guided by the deep desires God put in your heart.

The sky is vast and is the realm for all birds, but not all birds were designed for the same flight path. Neither is your path necessarily the same as the person next to you.

God has laid up a flight path just for you[7], and He wired you for success. Birds walk in their design by instinct. People walk away from their design by insecurity.

This chapter is the remedy to that misalignment.

Do you ever wonder about the capacity God equipped you with that you have yet to discover, let alone utilize? I submit that God gave us far more than He gave to birds[8]. After all, He made us in HIS image and HIS likeness[9].

When we walk in the full capacity that God designed us for in Christ, we will do great things, bear much fruit, and bring glory to God. We are invited to step into greatness, not for our glory, but for His.

Lean into your God-crafted design. Ask Him to make it plain to you.

Design reveals our purpose, but instinct and intuition teach you how to flow with it.

Step into Chapter Three to rediscover your inner superpower.

References: 1) Ephesians 2:6 2) Galatians 6:9 3) Romans 1:20 4) Romans 8:19
5) Ephesians 2:10 6) Ecclesiastes 9:11 + 1 Chronicles 12:32 7) Ephesians 2:10
8) Job 35:11 9) Genesis 1:26

CHAPTER 3

REDISCOVERING YOUR INNER SUPERPOWER

Instinct and Intuition

"Instinct and intuition beautify life because they free it."

Over the millennia, we have lost our understanding of, and reliance upon, our instincts and intuition. In doing so, we've left untouched and unharvested great swaths of our vast potential.

Consider birds for a moment… they come hardwired with instinct and intuition. We have that too. But in today's Western culture, those are often considered sub-par, unserious, primitive, unrefined impulses at odds with what we consider to be our superior powers of logic and reason. It's as if instinct and intuition are something that need to be tamped down, ignored, even denied. When, in fact, it was God who gave us those gifts, and they need to be recovered, developed, and honed, not ignored, or denied.

The beauty of them is that they rely on something that cannot be seen – an effortless wisdom. The kind that doesn't argue, doesn't analyze, and doesn't wait for permission. It simply knows.

Instinct is the native intelligence written into the very fabric of every living thing. The swallow doesn't go to flight school, yet it arcs through the sky with mathematical precision, seemingly enjoying every twist and turn with a flair we can only envy.

Do you remember the day and place of your birth? You only know because someone else told you. But the salmon, which never went to navigation school, instinctively finds its way hundreds of miles upstream to the very place of its birth. The newborn child turns instinctively toward the mother's breast. These are not learned responses. The programming came with the package.

We came into this world with more than a physical body. We came preloaded with an operating system that included intelligence, intuition, instinct, and an inner voice that uses intelligence to interpret and put into words what our intuition and instinct are telling us. When those "soft skills" are ignored, people struggle with their direction and purpose in life. They wonder if the thoughts they have are from God, themselves, or some outside spiritual entity. Birds don't have that struggle. They navigate life with the design and tools God gave them.

We, on the other hand, evaluate, deliberate, and cogitate, and all too often eliminate the inner guidance God designed us with – exchanging it for intellect, "logic," or the collective opinions of others, all of which are built on acquired but incomplete knowledge, often from dubious or unreliable sources.

Caveat: Logic which derives from Logos is a gift from God. If used properly, it displays wisdom, which Solomon said was the principal thing to acquire in life. However, logic is built with knowledge and if our knowledge is incomplete with respect to the matter we're deciding on, our logic can be faulty. Sometimes the "facts" we see, steer us to a faulty, but seemingly logical conclusion. For example... A deal looks solid, but your gut is telling you to turn it down. That's intuition kicking in. Hence the value of learning to tap into instinct and intuition.

In their purest form, instinct and intuition are pure harmony, a beautiful alignment with the unseen rhythm of life. Their voice echoes across your soul like a cool breeze on a warm day. You know you felt it, but aren't always sure where it came from or where it's leading. Your inner voice is the verbal interpreter inside you, where thought, emotion, and memory give words to what your intuition perceives, or even to what God's Spirit whispers.

Its purpose is to articulate the inner impression and give expression to what's happening in your heart. It is a translator, not an originator of ideas or impressions, providing useful language to help you and others, grasp the complexity and meaning of your instinct and intuition.

Instinct and intuition provide the subtle tug and quiet nudge that lead to life rather than struggle. They're not reckless; they're rooted in the design you came into this world with. And much like the vine that senses the direction of sunlight and climbs without hesitation, we have the innate ability to reach for what we cannot see, but know is there.

Instinct and intuition beautify life – because they free it.

When a creature moves by design, it does not strive; it simply flows. The gazelle's leap, the bird's migration, the flower's opening are all acts of obedience to an invisible script written by God. They are not random impulses, but willing participation in divine order. And when we rediscover the sanctity of our own God-given design that includes instinct and intuition, we can bypass the confusion of a myriad of external voices and begin to move again like God intended: gracefully, purposefully, and anxiety-free.

Our original design came preloaded with instinct and intuition, uncorrupted by fear, able to see and sense that which evades our five senses, freely offering insight and wisdom without words to guide us safely through life.

But the beautiful programming given to us by God got a virus called sin that can cause error in judgment and make trusting them alone unreliable. Hence the understandable hesitation to rely on them. There is, however, a remedy: the indwelling Spirit of God – Christ in us – that makes the glory God intended, within reach. But before I explain the significant advantage that gives us, allow me to clarify a few terms…

Instinct: Automatic Survival Reaction

Technically speaking, human instinct is hardwired, automatic behavior. It does not require conscious thought. It comes with your biology. You don't learn it… you inherit it for the purpose of preserving life and ensuring survival. For example: pulling your hand from a hot stove, a baby's reflex to suckle, or a person's sudden ducking response to a fast-moving object.

Intuition: Inner Directional Awareness

This is a type of "knowing" that comes without step-by-step reasoning. Intuition helps us discern what is true, reveals insight beyond mere logic, and assists in decision-making. It combines, in an instant, your past experiences with pattern recognition and spiritual sensitivity to give you an internal feeling or sense about a person or situation.

You might feel prompted not to trust a person even though you have no information about them to inform you otherwise. It may be what many call a gut feeling about a direction in business, or even a vacation choice. As invaluable as intuition is, it becomes a superpower when united with Christ in you. Colossians 3:15 tells us,

> "Let the peace of God rule in your hearts."

Notice the first word of that verse is "Let". It's a verb of permission, not compulsion, implying the peace of God is already present within. We don't manufacture His peace; we allow it to operate inside us.

When we let the Lord teach us to profit and lead us in the way we should go, He promises that our peace will flow like a river[1]. It's when we strive to succeed independent of Him that we experience anxiety, fear, and quite often, lack. Consider the instruction Paul gave us in Philippians 4:6–7:

> "Be anxious for nothing, but in everything by prayer and

> supplication, with thanksgiving, let your requests be made known to God; and the peace of God, which surpasses all understanding, will guard your hearts and minds through Christ Jesus."

When trials come or things don't seem to make sense to you, don't allow yourself to become anxious. Instead of focusing on what you don't have, or the severity of the problem, wrap your prayer (conversation with God) and supplications (heartfelt petitions for a particular need) in the language of thankfulness, because thankfulness creates a habitation for peace, whereas complaining and ingratitude do not.

Think of your heart for a moment as being like a morning glory flower that opens in the morning with the rising sun and then closes in the evening or as the day heats up. Only when it's open can it receive the light and allow pollination to occur. When your heart is darkened with worry or engaged in the heat of striving, it cannot receive what is freely available in the light of day.

When the peace of God floods your soul, it will far surpass your current understanding and stand guard over your heart and mind. While God is working on your behalf, you may never understand what really happened or how exactly God will deliver you, but that's okay, because you get the end result we all seek: peace of mind, and peace in your heart.

In 2009, my wife of 24 years was diagnosed with brain cancer, and 10 weeks later she succumbed to that illness. We fought it as hard as we knew how, but without success. For a full year after that loss, my heart was incessantly asking, "What happened?" I didn't understand how we lost that battle. One day, God asked me a question. He said, "Why do you want to know?"

I replied, "I want peace." He immediately responded, "My peace I give to you."

"But what happened?" I replied. I was trying to come to terms with my loss through intellectual, theological, and philosophical reasoning. Jesus simply replied again… "Why do you want to know?" "I need peace!" I replied with some desperation.

He gently spoke,

> "My peace I give to you; not as the world gives do I give to you."[2]

It was then that I realized, the peace I craved would not come through theological or intellectual means. It was supernatural, beyond my understanding. And it was beautiful. It was something to be received, not strived for. Then He directed me to Ephesians 4:17–18:

> "This I say, therefore, and testify in the Lord, that you should no longer walk as the rest of the Gentiles walk, in the futility of their mind, having their understanding darkened, being alienated from the life of God, because of the ignorance that is in them, because of the blindness of their heart."

I had been trying to apprehend peace in the futility of my mind, when what I needed only came by the Spirit, not the intellect.

The peace of God surpasses your understanding and goes well beyond the confusion you feel. Hebrews 4:11 tells us to "labor to enter into rest" (a benefit of peace). The best way I know to do that is to follow Paul's admonition in Philippians 4:8–9:

> "Finally, brethren, whatever things are true, whatever things are noble, whatever things are just, whatever things are pure,

> whatever things are lovely, whatever things are of good report, if there is any virtue and if there is anything praiseworthy – meditate on these things. The things which you learned and received and heard and saw in me, these do, and the God of peace will be with you."

The peace spoken of is not merely the cessation of strife or anxiety dependent upon circumstances. The Greek word for peace is *eirēnē*. It means to bind together that which was separated. It is literally the binding together of mind and spirit, heaven and earth, God and man, where nothing is missing, and nothing is broken.

This is the kind of peace that Jesus operated in during storms, betrayal, and ultimately the horror of the cross. More than the absence of conflict, it is a state of supernatural equilibrium, unaffected by the storms of life. It is the very atmosphere of Heaven finding expression within you.

The word translated *"rule"* is an athletic term often rendered as *umpire* or *referee*. It is the one who decides what counts and what doesn't, what's in play and what's out of bounds.

The peace of God might prompt you to stop and opt out even when everything looks good. Conversely, it may urge you to step forward even when circumstances or people advise otherwise. Think of it as a governing presence that makes a ruling, impresses it upon your spirit, yet leaves the choice up to you.

The problem often is that we haven't developed the habit of waiting on God, stilling the noise and traffic of our minds and outside voices, and wading prayerfully into Scripture (the living *logos* of God) to let it speak to our hearts.

When we develop the habit of fellowshipping with God in Spirit and

Word, His voice becomes familiar, easily identifiable among many others. I can pick my wife's voice out of a crowd because of the depth of time I've spent with her over the years. Not only do I recognize her voice effortlessly, but even without hearing it, I know her preferences without her being present.

The same is true with the Lord. The more time you spend with Him, anchored in His Word, and nourished by His Spirit, the more readily you recognize His promptings and know His preferences for your life.

Our heart, of course, is the control center, the intersection of thought, desire, and spiritual perception, where decisions are made, motives are born, and God's Spirit communes with ours. It's a well-accepted belief in the sales profession that 90% of any buyer's decision is made in the heart and 10% resides in the mind. Essentially, the heart decides what it wants, and the mind negotiates the best terms it can get.

When the peace of God rules in our heart, it doesn't just quiet competing voices; it governs our choices, informs our responses, and awakens our perceptions. When you *let* that peace rule in your heart, the long shadows of fear, doubt, and conflict slip away.

While human intuition is the capacity to "just know" something without analytical reasoning, it can often be flawed due to our interpretation of past events. Paul tells us that we can be renewed in the spirit of our mind, so we don't have to rely on the futility of our natural mind, with understanding darkened by ignorance and blindness of heart[3]. As believers in Jesus Christ, we can employ flawless spiritual intuition birthed out of union with the Spirit of God.

In effect, when you let the peace of God rule in your heart, you are calibrating your natural intuitive sense to the divine presence of God within. That's something you can trust completely.

Think of the peace of God as being to your natural intuition what a tuning fork is to a piano. When you *let* the peace of God rule in your heart, it subtly adjusts and aligns your natural intuition into union with Him. You can tell when something just feels right, not because it necessarily makes sense, but because, like a dove, it simply rests within you.

The peace of God doesn't shout; it whispers to your spirit, giving you an inner sense or nudge in a certain direction. As you yield to that peace, it creates a knowing that exceeds words, a conviction that withstands testing, and a certainty that defies explanation.

We all have an inner voice that originates from within, it pushes outward from our thoughts. It is how the conscious mind interprets inner knowing. It often speaks in words, impressions, or moral promptings: "Don't do that," "Call this person," "That's not right."

But there is another voice: the voice of God within the believer. He speaks only truth, and He does so by His Spirit[5]. While natural intuition arises from the soul in the form of thoughts, the voice of God (what you might call spiritual intuition) arises from union with the Spirit of God in your heart. It's like you sense it in your belly. The point of origination is not the mind. It is not a random thought. It emerges from your innermost being. As Jesus said,

> "He who believes in Me, as the Scripture has said, out of his belly will flow rivers of living water"[5].

Some translations say, "out of his heart," referring to the innermost part of our being rather than the mind.

Not all intuition is of God. Human intuition can be distorted by fear, pride, or past experience. But when the peace of God reigns within the heart, it purifies the signal, aligning human perception with divine guidance. That's why Scripture links peace with discernment:

> "The wisdom that is from above is first pure, then peaceable…"[6].

Heaven's wisdom doesn't create confusion; it creates calm. True intuition, flowing from a heart ruled by peace, bears the signature of Heaven: clarity without tension, confidence without striving.

A Practical Picture

Imagine a bird gliding on an unseen thermal. It doesn't calculate the wind's equations; it feels the lift. That lift is like the peace of God, invisible but sustaining. The bird's instinct to ride it, mirrors intuition, sensing where invisible support is strongest.

In the same way, when your spirit lives in peace, your intuition can catch the movements of the Spirit, rising effortlessly on divine currents instead of flapping in human effort.

When peace rules the heart, intuition becomes the interpreter of Heaven's whispers.

There is a power you can tap into, little discussed but highly effective and modeled by birds. Turn to Chapter 4 to learn how to discover the power of Framing Your Day.

References: 1) Isaiah 48:17–18 2) John 14:27 3) Ephesians 4:17–18, 23 4) John 4:24 5) John 7:38 6) James 3:17

CHAPTER 4

FRAME YOUR DAY

The Dawn Chorus

"Birds start their day with purpose. They begin with declaration. They wake the world with intention"

In March of 2015, my wife and I were staying at the Dan Jerusalem Hotel in Israel. It was her second trip to the Holy Land, but my first. The room was wonderful, a welcome refuge after traveling from Florida to New York, then Tel Aviv, and finally Jerusalem. We went to bed late, expecting to sleep in the next morning, something my wife Judy does quite naturally.

She is not accustomed to seeing the sunrise, though she has heard about it. Our first morning there was different. Judy awoke before dawn and, lying quietly in bed, began to pray for Israel, for our adventure ahead, and for whom we might bless while there.

Then, around 4:30 AM, before the first line of gold touched the rim of the eastern sky, something otherworldly broke the night's silence. The peace that had been our companion gave way to the sound of angels, otherwise known as house sparrows. It was the "dawn chorus".

Not wanting to wake me, Judy slipped quietly out of bed, opened the bathroom window, and recorded the rapturous sound of a hundred tiny creatures joyfully awakening the dawn with their song.

Imagine my surprise when I awoke to find Judy out of bed, camera in hand, beaming at me with the biggest smile, fully awake and completely tuned in to the moment. She quoted Psalm 57:7–11:

"My heart, O God, is steadfast, my heart is steadfast; I will sing and make music. Awake, my soul! Awake, harp and lyre! ***I will awaken the dawn***. I will praise you, Lord, among the nations; I will sing of you among the peoples. For great is your love, reaching to the heavens; your faithfulness reaches to the skies. Be exalted, O God, above the heavens; let your glory be over all the earth."

She had seen it all, from the moment when darkness had not yet lifted and the light had not yet won, when it seemed as though the city itself was holding its breath, to the moment when that first bird broke the silence with one solitary note.

That first note was not a random clearing of the throat. It was an invitation to every other bird to join the chorus and declare the day. Needing no further encouragement, perhaps hundreds of birds joined in, full-throated, as if their song was somehow pulling the sun above the horizon so the rest of the world could awaken.

It was like they saw the light of the coming day as a gift from God and could not wait for everyone else to bask in it, so they sang it forward. Waking the dawn with song is not a new thing. Psalm 104:19 - 24 tells us that creation awakens daily in an orderly rhythm set by God Himself.

"He made the moon to mark the seasons. The sun knows its time for setting... When the sun rises, man goes out to work."

Singing is tied explicitly to creation itself. When God asked Job 75 consecutive questions[1] meant to give him perspective, He asked,

"Where were you when I laid the foundation of the earth... When the morning stars sang together, and all the sons of God shouted for joy?"[2]

Creation itself began with a song. Greeting the day with song is a gift to us, for us, and even through us, if we choose it. Psalm 19 tells us that the heavens have no speech nor words, yet their voice goes out through all the earth[3]. Creation speaks despite having no language of words. Creation indeed has a message, but it is not limited to, or defined by words alone.

As wondrous as the dawn chorus of birds is, it's not optional for them. In Psalm 148, God explicitly commands birds to praise the Lord. But singing in the morning is not the exclusive domain of birds. Psalm 59:16 declares,

> "I will sing of Your strength. I will sing aloud of Your steadfast love in the morning."

My wife breaks into song throughout the day. It comes so naturally to her. When I hear her voice floating in the air, I stop what I'm doing and drink it in.

David did not wait for the dawn to awaken him. Like the birds, he woke the dawn. In Scripture, sound precedes creation. God spoke, and it was so[4]. With birds, song precedes activity. They seem to understand something as old as time itself. They give voice to the day before they begin their work.

If you read the science books, you will often find the dawn chorus described as birds defining their territory or attracting a mate. But there is more to it. They sing in part, to wake themselves up. It floods their brains with dopamine, those "feel good" chemicals that sharpen the mind and bring the body into rhythm. It is biology tuning its instrument.

For many birds, they're not coming out with their best performance. Their singing is not ready for prime time, so the early morning music festival becomes their practice hall. It's where they learn their songs through repetition. It's where today's faltering attempts, drowned out by everyone else's song, become tomorrow's mastery.

The song of the bird is its signature in sound, a declaration of identity where every note marks territory, demonstrates competence to potential mates, and establishes an unquestionable presence. Like the Irishman who joined William Wallace in the movie Braveheart and referred to Ireland as "my island," birds announce their presence saying in effect, I'm right here. This place is mine.

In Psalm 12:4, David laments that faithfulness to God has nearly disappeared, and then he quotes the ungodly who boast,

> "With our tongue we will prevail."

I believe they were saying in effect, "We'll prevail by controlling the narrative." And he who controls the narrative controls the nation. Perhaps you're not in a position to affect the social narrative, but you can control the narrative you allow into your consciousness. What we allow in, is what comes out, and that ultimately sets the tone for the day.

When you hear birds singing, you're hearing the sound of projected confidence, because birds don't sing when they feel threatened.

Birds do not wait for the day or those in it to tell them who they are. They announce at the first hint of light who they are. Like any high performer in life, they set their intent before checking emails or responding to social media notifications. They choose identity driven action, the kind of behavior that flows naturally from a clear sense of who or what they are.

Most people flow instead from urgency-driven reaction, behavior shaped by circumstances, pressures, scarcity, comparison, or fear of missing out. Birds have a simple habit. Before the day lays its demands on them, they confidently declare their identity, territory, and intentions.

Before you get wrapped up in the news or your inbox, declare your identity to the world. Not literally to the world, but in reality, more to yourself than anyone else. You have to take territory internally before you can hope to take territory externally. Your song or declaration is your leadership signal. It is you raising the flag in the morning. If you don't do it, someone else will shape your day for you. For me, Scripture is both grounding and uplifting. I remind myself that...

> "I am accepted in the beloved[5], greatly loved by my Father in heaven[6], and able to do all things through Christ who strengthens me[7], because greater is He that is in me than he who is in the world[8]".

Amidst the throng of maestros, comes another sound known as "call notes", short and sharp context specific communications that keep the flock connected, coordinate movement, indicate readiness, and may even communicate a mild alert rather than an impending threat. These notes aren't a song. They're declarations of alignment that keep everyone on the same page of awareness, including signaling where food has been found or simply touching base with others in the flock.

Joining the morning chorus is a third and often overlooked category of song called "subsong". Think of a five-year-old child singing a solo at a Christmas pageant. Essentially, "subsong" is the youngest of birds trying to imitate and learn from their parents, singing the same tunes while still learning. That sound can be rough when they first begin.

If you are in a place of learning right now, take a cue from the birds and practice your future in private before taking it public. To minimize embarrassment and enhance success, practice alone, or on small stages. High achievers in any field practice who they are becoming, not who they have been in the past. Before extraordinary performance, there is always consistent, ordinary practice.

The people who outperform are more often than not
the people who out practice everyone else.

King David was an accomplished warrior, but he was not born with those skills. They had to be developed. He had to train. He recognized that as he trained, it was God working in him. He said in Psalm 144:1,

> "Blessed be the Lord my Rock, who trains my hands for war, and my fingers for battle."

That level of training went down to the detail of his fingers. How much practice are you putting into becoming what you believe God has in store for you. God does a work in you before He unveils to the world what He has placed in you, but that always requires your willing participation.

The scientific foundation that made it all make sense to me
When we wake up, the first thirty to sixty minutes are special. Our brains are relaxed and more open to new ideas. The thinking part of your brain is slower to come online, but the emotional part is already active. This means what you tell yourself in this window of time penetrates deeply and shapes not only your feelings, but also what you expect for the day and how you will handle whatever good or bad the day may bring.

Here is the remarkable part
When you speak out loud, a part of your brain called the "Reticular Activating System" (RAS) becomes engaged. Your RAS works like a spotlight, highlighting what you decide is important and filtering out

background noise. When you start talking about what matters to you, you begin seeing it everywhere. Opportunities, ideas, solutions, and open doors start standing out. What you repeat, becomes what remains.

What you focus on expands

For example, when you decide it's time to buy a new vehicle and choose a certain make and model, you suddenly notice them everywhere. They were always there, but you didn't notice them because they weren't important at the time. Your senses take in millions of bits of data per second, but your conscious mind can only process a tiny fraction. Your RAS decides what gets through by filtering it through one question... Is this important to you right now?

Your RAS tags what you care about as relevant, moving it from background noise to foreground awareness, which is why it feels like they're suddenly everywhere, but in reality, the only thing that changed was your perception. RAS does NOT manifest anything. It's just a high-level filter designed by God for your benefit.

When you speak hopeful, faith filled words about your direction, you train your brain to notice anything that matches those words. Instead of locking on to what could hold you back, you begin seeing what will move you forward. In practical terms, you steer your brain toward behaviors that help you realize your goals.

Birds sing in the morning not because they're bored, but because dawn is the most neurologically and ecologically strategic moment of their day. Their song sets the tone for behavior and interaction and even affects the atmosphere of the flock. What you speak with intention in the morning can have the same effect for you.

Morning declarations work because when you first wake up, the boundary between conscious and subconscious is thin, and your brain is still relaxed. Your words slip past the rational mind and plant deeply in the soil of belief. In this brief window, what you speak with purpose, becomes the roadmap your day will follow.

Your Reticular Activating System takes those words as instructions and decides what to notice or ignore and which opportunities to draw to your attention. Meanwhile, the planning centers of your brain, begin aligning with what you said matters. Behavior then changes. You begin acting like the person you told yourself you were. Identity strengthens, anxiety weakens, and goal-oriented actions increase almost effortlessly because you're following a script already written.

Wearing a breastplate of fiery orange, the robin raises its voice in the cool morning air, inviting others to join the melody. Moments later, a few sparrows heed the call, spraying the air with musical notes no human musician could replicate. Not to be outdone, a red bird threads a piercing whistle through the trees in a repeated pattern, as though announcing something of high importance.

When you hear that sound, you intuitively sense its message is intentional, a message not meant for us, yet one that is nevertheless instructive. It's a masterclass in leadership, communication, intention, and even success, an intelligence briefing of sorts, held in the open for all to hear.

Declare Your Identity Before the World Defines It for You

The American robin is abundant throughout North America and renowned for rising early to break the silence of the night. It does not clear its throat, warm up, or test the air. It simply starts. Out comes a bold, confident call to attention, not the least bit concerned about what the owl thinks of it, or whether the nightingale has a wider range.

Before the world pronounces its assessment,
the robin has already announced who it is.

We would do well to begin our days knowing the same, not with an ego inflated sense of self, but with a simple proclamation of who God made us to be – carriers of His presence, shaped in His image, and bearers of His likeness. Paul said it plainly in Galatians 3:26...

> "For you are all sons of God through faith in Christ Jesus."

Maybe start with that. When we shrink back from the truth, we deny ourselves the framework of identity we need in order to find and fulfill our destiny.

The robin sings before it sees provision. Before any evidence of food appears, it sings. Just as faith precedes breakthrough, the song of the robin precedes supply. The lesson is simple...

> Life tends to reward those who show up early and expectantly,
> with a song in their heart and ready hands.

Successful entrepreneurs do this intuitively. They know what they are building, why it matters, who they serve, and the value it will deposit into the lives of everyone affected. They show up early because it's usually the first voice of the day that sets the tone and direction for what follows.

Robins have an incredible ability to detect worms beneath the ground, sensing movement that most creatures miss. They listen for what others do not notice, discerning opportunity beneath the surface long before it rises into view. That is the hallmark of every successful person, noticing the signals of provision hidden below the surface, then taking the necessary action to seize it.

Read the Environment Before Taking Action

The Song Sparrow is so plain in appearance it can almost go unnoticed, and so small in stature it can be dismissed as insignificant, yet this little masterpiece carries one of the most intricate vocal repertoires in the bird world. It improvises like a jazz musician in a jam session, while composing like Beethoven or Bach. Its enthusiasm comes across like a worshiper lost in praise.

Just as Jesus Christ, the Son of God, clothed Himself in unremarkable form, with no beauty that we should desire Him[9], God loves to hide His best gifts in humble packages. What truly stands out about the sparrow is not only its captivating song, but its awareness.

Each morning, like a concert pianist testing every note until he feels it, the sparrow listens between the notes, gauging humidity, temperature, and wind, all of which affect how sound travels. The sparrow is doing something more than fine tuning its song. It is reading the day, evaluating conditions before committing energy to the task.

Successful people do the same. They check their internal state before they speak, confirm their schedule before they sprint, notice subtle shifts others miss, and read between the lines in conversation.

What you hear in the quiet becomes
what you release in the open.

Identify Threats Before They Surface – One of the most sophisticated communicators in the forest is the boldly curious black capped chickadee, small in stature but large in importance. It is known for its distinctive call, "chickadee-dee-dee-dee-dee-dee", which is not a bird with a stutter. It is a coded threat assessment.

A single soft call is calming and signifies all is well, but a longer string of "dees" signals approaching danger. If delivered in a rapid burst, it's as if the bird has pulled the fire alarm, and there's a predator nearby. As the dawn chorus begins, chickadees listen intently to each other, counting the "dees" and listening for intensity, mapping threats before the day fully begins. Their vigilance saves lives. The lesson is clear,

Neutralize risk before it becomes a problem.

In business, think of it as neutralizing friction before it derails your day. Scan early for signs of trouble. Identify bottlenecks. Name the fears that paralyze you. Have the conversations you need to gain clarity on looming threats. The more you think ahead, the more you reduce risk and minimize the impact of any lurking crisis.

Walk in Peace – The mourning dove embodies the message of peace. Its easy posture, soft colors, and gentle cooing have made it a symbol of calm from time immemorial. In Matthew 10:16, Jesus sent His disciples out with the admonition to be "wise as serpents and **harmless as doves**". Doves avoid danger rather than engage it, which requires discernment, awareness, and attentiveness. They demonstrate that not everyone is a warrior in the same way, some people prevail by trusting their God given discernment and stepping out of the way of trouble.

Doves refuse the bait, not because they are weak, but because they value inner peace. Peace on the inside leads to better decisions than ones made in the heat of battle.

Build Harmony and Emotional Stability Within Your Flock – In the early morning light, before the forest is fully awake, the song of the wood thrush floods the woodland with what sounds like a magic flute. It travels through the trees like light spilling through branches, with tones no other bird can produce.

Many birds have two voice boxes, but the wood thrush belongs to a rare category that can sing two notes at the same time, creating harmonies that calm the woodland. When it sings, tensions drop, nervous wings rest, and the forest exhales. Likewise, your internal harmony, or your inner turbulence, becomes the atmosphere of your flock, your team, your family, your congregation. Emotionally steady leaders calm the people around them, just as a parent who holds peace, anchors a household. Carrying calm in trials is not optional for leaders, it's a requirement.

The thrush sings, not because life is easy,
but because it is precious.

Reset Your Inner World Before Engaging the Outer One – I'm a public person. I speak, teach, train, and consult for a living. But when I'm not in that mode, I prefer separation from hustle and noise. I do not care about crowded beaches or long lines at amusement parks. I want to go where silence is interrupted only by the sound of birds, wind in the trees, or rushing water.

There is a bird much like that, a species that seems made for holy quiet. While other birds sing relentlessly, the hermit thrush sings in phrases. First the melody, then space, then a tone, then more silence, as though it is listening to its own notes echo through the forest.

The hermit thrush is sometimes called the monk of the forest because it withdraws into ravines and glades where noise does not follow. This is not loneliness. Think of it as consecration, because...

Some revelations come only in solitude.

Its message is to go deeper, get quieter, and trust the inner leading of God's Spirit, because your true calling is often found while waiting in stillness. So tomorrow, when you rise, before you take on the day's challenges, begin to declare the day, not timidly, but with confidence. Before you see provision, act with expectancy, without demanding evidence or guarantees. Respond to the path before you, with trust in God. Begin with faith, not fear. Choose confidence, not concern. Proceed with anticipation, not hesitation.

Birds sing the dawn chorus to align their lives, calibrate direction, and set the course of destiny. Each day they follow a simple routine**, sing, seek, and secure.** Their success is not the result of one grand act, but of consistent alignment with purpose, day after day.

The Power of Words – An Important Clarification

Words matter... Which is why David prayed that the words of his mouth would be acceptable in God's sight... (Psalm 19:14) That also implies that some words may not be acceptable to God. This brings me to an idea gaining popularity, the claim that you can manifest anything by decreeing and declaring it to be so. The idea is that your words, if spoken with the right tone, vibration, and duration, can manifest anything your little ol' heart desires.

Some Christians base their idea on Job 22:28 which in some translations reads, "You will also declare a thing, And it will be established for you". The Hebrew word translated "declare" should be translated as "decide". In other words, it should read, "You will **decide a matter** and it will be established." That's true because you can't establish what you've not decided upon.

This ancient idea, originating from Egyptian beliefs in Memphite Theology and Babylonian "Mardukian" beliefs, was a major tenant of Gnosticism that plagued the early church. They taught that you could unlock great power by knowing and speaking the *right words*. It was an ancient version of what some now call, "name it and claim it". Speech to them, was a *mechanism* that wielded great power which they believed was stored within, and merely had to be unlocked by saying the secret words in the right way. It was all up to you.

Nearly 100 years ago, William Branham revived and rebranded this gnostic idea, cloaking it with misapplied Scripture claiming he had literally spoken squirrels into existence while hunting one day in Kentucky. This idea assumes power originates in the self, but Jesus said, "I can of Myself do nothing".[10] Jesus, the very Son of God, who was and is, the Word of God[11], went on to say that He did nothing on His own authority, and only spoke what the Father taught Him[12], and only did what He saw the Father doing[13].

The core fault of this manifestation craze is that it assumes the power within you, is waiting to be unleashed in any direction you choose. A very attractive idea to many. It's so God-like, but we are not God. Even Jesus famously said, "Not My will, but Thine be done.[14]" Who are we to think we should do otherwise?

At best, any result from such an effort becomes what Paul described as wood, hay, and stubble to be burned up on that Day[15]. Why pursue that which will be burned up?

Of course, I realize Paul said that Christ in us is our hope of glory[16]. But Jesus is not some magic genie we unleash to do *our will* with some Christian version of "Abradadabra" (which is ancient Aramaic, meaning, "I create as I speak"). And yes, I know that life and death are in the power of the tongue[17], but that doesn't mean words magically turn sound into substance.

Here's how words create life and death... For example, they can generate life-giving faith or instill life-depleting fear. Romans 10:17 says that "faith comes by hearing". In order for faith to come by hearing, words must be spoken. Words can also inspire hope or instill despair. They can build trust or arouse suspicion. A soft answer turns away wrath: but grievous words stir up anger[18]. Words in that way are powerful, but they don't turn sound into substance.

Use your words to crystalize or clarify your intentions if for no one else but yourself. When I set my intention for the day with something like, "Today, I plan to finish this manuscript, or make X number of recordings", it focuses me on the goal for the day. Otherwise, I tend to spend my day in reaction mode rather than being proactive. This matters because spoken words tend to stimulate emotions. Emotions fuel desire, desire provides motivation, motivation prompts decision, decision leads to behavior, behavior generates results, and results deliver rewards. See Ultimate Success Framework flywheel below...

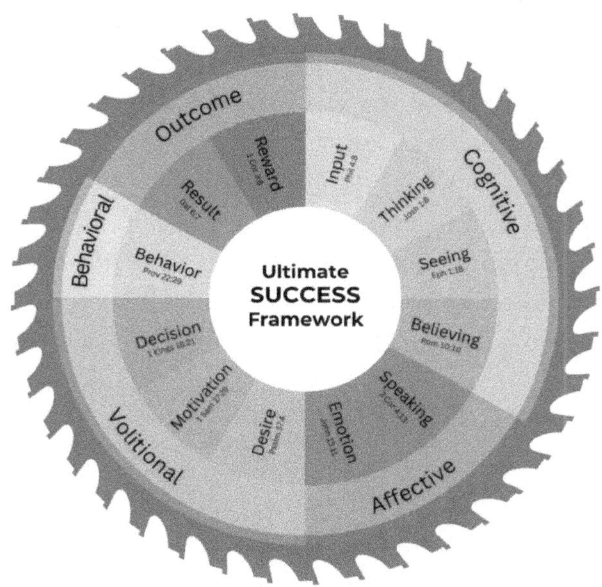

Spoken declarations are helpful to be sure, but they don't have the same physiological regulatory effect on the nervous system that powerful singing does. Here's why...When you simply speak a declaration, the analytical side of your mind can and most likely will, evaluate it, raise questions about it, even doubt its veracity and in the end resist it. But when you sing, the rhythm, melody, and cadence do an end run around resistance and go straight to the emotional, subconscious brain to deposit truth deeper than speaking alone will.

Singing is a God-Designed Tool For Transformation

Over and over again in Scripture, we are commanded to sing psalms, hymns and spiritual songs[19]. We read in Zephaniah that God Himself will "rejoice over you with singing.[20]" Paul and Silas sang, and the prison doors opened[21]. God delivered Israel when Jehoshaphat appointed singers to go in front of the army to ward off the attackers[22], and promises to surround us with "songs of deliverance"[23]. Clearly, singing is important to God. He does it for us, over us and through us.

Venture into the flower-filled meadows of Europe on any Spring morning before the sun has had the chance to soak up the morning dew from the grass, while the horizon is still deciding whether to allow the sun above its brim, and you will witness one of nature's most astonishing spectacles... the Eurasian Skylark.

Not much to look at really, plain brown with a light underbelly, nothing to really grab your attention. That is, until it suddenly launches... not at prey or some morsel of food. It launches vertically like a rocket leaving the launch pad and it begins to sing and sing and sing and sing.

It keeps climbing higher and higher with its wings beating furiously, his body straining against the pull of gravity, and all the while his song becomes more robust, somehow brighter, and more extravagant and unrestrained with every inch of elevation.

Rising into the sky is a battle against gravity, but the skylark shows that...

You rise the highest when you sing
in the midst of the struggle.

When my wife of 24 years passed away, the grief was unbearable. I would find the most uplifting worship music of the era, blast it loud and sing my heart out, with tears flowing down my face. And somehow in the song, I got healing I could find nowhere else.

The key here is to sing during the climb out of the pit, to sing when the night is still dark, and daylight seems to be held in ransom. Don't wait until after the victory. Don't postpone your song until after the breakthrough.

Your song is the breakthrough!

It's your victory. Joy is not just the result of the climb out of the pit, joy is the fuel for your rising up again. When trouble comes, and Jesus promised it would[24], rise in song... don't run in defeat.

When you start each day, your mind has yet to claim any territory, your emotions are likely at neutral, and your spirit is awaiting direction. Your business has battles to win, and your day is still formless. If you don't claim your internal territory through declaration, your environment will claim it for you, and you will be led by the tyranny of the urgent, and the unbridled emotions within, instead of the vision God has for you.

Birds don't succumb to emotions or disappointment. They declare their intentions with clarity. Our lives need the same vocal intention.

Dawn alignment calibrates direction, but direction becomes destiny only through small, consistent action. Birds understand this... every day they follow the same rhythm: ***sing, seek, secure***. Their success is not in a single dramatic effort, but in steady, repeated motion.

Step into Chapter Five to discover how daily foraging becomes a powerful blueprint for business, leadership, and spiritual fruitfulness.

References: 1) Job 38 – 41 2) Job 38:4, 7 3) Psalm 19:3-4 4) Genesis 1:3 5) Ephesians 1:6 6) Ephesians 2:4 7) Philippians 4:13 8) 1 John 4:4 9) Isaiah 53:2 10) John 5:30 11) John 1:1 12) John 8:28 13) John 5:19 14) Luke 22:42 15) 1 Corinthians 3:12-13 16) Colossians 1:27 17) Proverbs 18:21 18) Proverbs 15:1 19) Ephesians 5:29 20) Zephaniah 3:17 21) Acts 16:25-26 22) 2 Chronicles 20:21-22 23) Psalm 32:7 24) John 16:33

CHAPTER 5

THE HOLY HABIT OF CONSISTENT ACTION

Daily Foraging

"Focusing on one thing produces mastery,
but divided attention leads to lack."

God does not leave the supply of food for birds up to chance. He has hardwired them with practical wisdom, fitted to their design, to successfully find the provision they need, that He has already set aside for them.

Imagine the complexity of feeding 50 billion birds each day, across eleven thousand distinct species, all feeding from only fifty to seventy distinct food categories. What is fascinating, is that God did not create eleven thousand menus, one for each species. There are not an infinite number of provision types. There are several dozen. That's it.

Thousands of species share the same food strategies, but they do it in different places, at different sizes, and with varied methods. Provision is finite, but the ways to access that provision show virtually endless variety in design.

Birds begin their day with song,
but they build their life with work.

Not fear driven work. Not greed motivated work. Not stress filled work. Just steady, faithful, persistent, and at times innovative work, carried out daily. They are not stretched out on the sofa in their nest waiting for God to throw provision their way. The provision they require is outside the nest, and they know how to find it.

Consistency produces sufficiency
Birds don't buy lottery tickets, nor are they creatures of luck. What they are is a masterclass in *habitual practices* that produce consistent, reliable results. Sufficiency doesn't mean just having enough to scrape by, nor does it mean living in opulence. Paul describes Biblical sufficiency as having enough for every good work[1]. That will vary depending on one's calling, vision, and belief.

The osprey is often considered one of the greatest work ethic birds on the planet, a creature of productive habit. Many ospreys will fish the same lake, bay, or stretch of river, often at the exact same time of day, and some even use the same perch from which to spot fish below. The osprey is successful because it has ***become a master of one thing***, and it does that one thing with remarkable consistency.

Its success rate is nearly one in four dives, which is exceptional in the animal world. It may not catch a fish on its first few dives, but it knows that if it keeps diving, it will have fish for dinner.

Success comes more from repeatable
routines than random attempts.

The question you may want to ask is this, what skill or activity can you compound through consistent practice, something the market values, that can set you in a category of one? Focusing on one thing produces mastery, but divided attention leads to lack.

God provides the conditions and environment,
but birds gather the provision.

When we see birds soaring gracefully, we're witnessing the result of disciplined, consistent work that happened before, and between, those moments of beauty. They begin their day with a knowing that they will be fed, then they act on that "knowing" consistently, demonstrating what James 2:17 says, that "faith without works is dead".

The secret to the bird's worry-free life of never-ending provision is their daily habit of foraging for what God has made available. They go into the forest knowing provision is there. All they have to do is find and gather what God has stored up for them. For them, it's a treasure hunt every day. I'm guessing they love doing it.

Do the common thing uncommonly well, and do it consistently

If you want to succeed in life, you don't have to invent the next big thing or start the next viral craze. Every day, do the fundamentals, and do them with excellence. Robins have been foraging for worms the same way since the beginning. Provision is found in faithfully performing the basics. It's not rocket science or mystical. It's fundamental.

The bulk of a bird's waking hours are dedicated to foraging. This is not glamorous. It's not like the graceful soaring or melodic calls that capture our attention. But it is the foundation that makes everything else possible.

Walk along the beach and you will probably see a sandpiper making hundreds of darting probes each hour. Its success depends on consistent effort. It's nonstop. It knows that if it keeps at it, adjusting as necessary with the movement of the tide and the prey beneath the sand, it will be well fed. It never fails. Plus, they get to enjoy beach life.

God creates the environment, and the sandpiper knows it is up to it to locate the prey and feast. It was created for this. It's their design, even its calling. Similarly, the robin searching for worms in your backyard is following its design, and in doing so, does not lack provision.

Let this sink in. Why does the sandpiper go to the beach to feed, but never to your backyard? Why does the robin never go to the beach, where there is clearly an abundance of food? Does the robin envy the sandpiper? Does the eagle flying overhead envy either of them? No. In simple terms, they know their lane and stay in it. Your provision is in the lane God has for you. If you try to forage in the lane suited for someone else, you may go hungry, or if you are fed, it will not satisfy.

When you're in the right lane,
your work feels like nourishment.

You might be exhausted by your work, but you're also deeply satisfied. Robins eat worms because they are nourished by them, not because it's a glamorous career. Ask yourself whether the work you're doing drains you or satisfies you. If you need *constant*, external motivation, you're probably in the wrong lane.

You can often find your lane by recognizing what unresolved problems bother you, and noticing that you feel equipped to help solve them. Here is another clue... What comes out of you under pressure? What abilities surface under fire?

Pressure reveals design more clearly than comfort does. Jesus pointed out that there are shepherds who, when pressure comes, run because they're really hirelings. Are you doing work only for the paycheck, work you will abandon the moment difficulty arrives? If so, it may be best to make a change now. What do others notice in you and draw from you, even when you're not trying? What do people regularly thank you for, or come to you for, without you prompting them? What do you give that costs you little, but rewards others greatly?

Another indicator relates to faith. The choice in front of you may feel risky and require courage. That can be a good thing. But if it requires you to silence your conscience or compromise your values, that's a deal breaker. Faith will stretch you, but compromise and misalignment will fracture you.

Will the lane you're considering still appeal to you in the daily grind? Some people love welding and do it every day in harsh conditions. Others only see the possible income and eventually hate their job, and even their life. Find work that fulfills you even when no one notices, the kind of work you would do for free if you could.

Here is a clue... A robin does not wake up and decide it wants to be a robin. It simply is. Your job is to see what flows best with your inner and outer design, then do that. In Sarasota there is a young couple who started a sandwich shop called ***Focaccia Sandwich and Bakery.*** They make the best sandwiches in town and are always slammed. When I stop in to see how they're doing, even though they're busier than a one-legged butt kicker in a butt kicking contest, they have the biggest smiles. They genuinely enjoy what they do.

Your lane is most likely where you are nourished, not drained, where you notice problems you can solve, that others overlook, where your true strengths surface under fire, where people are regularly helped by you, and where it fits you like a glove. It is part of God's calling on your life, even if only for a season.

Let's talk about that last phrase, "even if only for a season" ... God may open a door of provision for you in the form of a job. If you believe God brought you there, then in my opinion you stay until He releases you, not merely until you don't like it anymore, or until the boss treats you unfairly.

When I moved to America from Canada, God pointed out a place where I was to work. I got the job and was promoted a couple of times, but during that two-year period I had run ins with the executive vice president. He told me that mixing faith and business would not be allowed and found other ways to get under my skin. We nearly came to physical blows one day in his office, both of us red faced and fists clenched. Not a good look for me, I know.

My wife told me they did not deserve me and that I should find another job where I would be appreciated, even celebrated. You may have heard the expression, "Go where you're celebrated, not where you're tolerated," but that's bad theology. Thank God, Jesus did not subscribe to that. He came to His own and His own did not receive Him. He didn't just go somewhere else where people might be nicer.

I told my wife that God directed me to work there, so I had to stay until He said I could leave. I would serve at my highest level until that time. Even though I nearly came to blows with the executive vice president, my job was reasonably secure, because the team I was responsible for increased sales by 430 percent after I took over.

Then there came a day when one of the sales reps I managed was supposed to meet me back at the office for a review around two or three in the afternoon. I arranged my schedule, but he did not show up until just after five. Needless to say, I was ticked, especially when he admitted he had not forgotten the appointment. He had simply been out driving around.

As I ushered him into my office, I intended to land on him pretty hard for that disregard and irresponsibility. But as I closed the door for confidentiality, the Holy Spirit interrupted my intentions and simply, and firmly said, "MERCY."

My response was as quick as it was wrong. "Mercy? He doesn't deserve mercy!" But the Lord replied just as quickly, "And neither did you, but before he leaves your office, he will be born again, and you will be free to leave the company."

Sure enough, I took an entirely different approach. I was kind and inquisitive, and ultimately led him in a prayer of salvation, and he was genuinely born again. That was my indicator that I was free to leave, and I was gone within weeks. I tell you that story because I view my life as an assignment from God. It's not only about what I want. When I do what He assigns, I have found there is abundant provision.

Another example

A company reached out to me decades ago to see if I could help them with sales. They had been stuck at $22 million in annual revenue for three years and wanted to break out. I did what I always do, a three-day onsite analysis. However, the executive vice president and I did not hit it off, and on my flight home I decided to pass on giving them a training proposal.

But here is where your will is only part of the process. As I prayed on the flight home, I decided I didn't want to work with them because of that one man. However, God interrupted my thinking and said, "He's your assignment." I replied, "Then there are no quantity pricing discounts. They will pay full price!"

It became my highest paying contract up to that point, and God was glorified in many ways. I was able to be a witness to roughly seventy sales personnel, and even though I began mid-year, we blew through their previous records and topped $30 million in revenue. I did not want the opportunity going into it, but I recognized the lane God was directing me into, where I was skilled and could bring impact, and I was well rewarded in the process.

With those caveats out of the way, let me return to foraging. Most birds forage between four and eight hours a day, depending on species. Generally speaking, the larger the bird, the less time it spends actively foraging. Eagles may spend only one to three hours actively hunting, but they spend many more hours observing the landscape, soaring above it, and waiting for the opportune moment to strike. Sometimes, when work gets hectic for me, I think of the eagle soaring, and close my eyes to allow my mind and heart to envision soaring in heavenly places that Paul spoke of in Ephesians 2:6, bringing calm, peace, and perspective before resuming my work.

Regardless of routine, they don't rush or panic. They align their actions with their design and, day after day, do the same things in largely the same ways, and consistently receive the reward they seek. If you look around, perhaps even in the mirror, you may see someone who is inconsistent with the small things that bring provision. They get inspired, often starting strong but lack the drive and vision to maintain the pace and see it through.

When I began my copier sales career in January of 1976, I understood that if I was going to succeed in sales, I had to master the basics. The idea of a sales career inspired me, and the money motivated me, but if I wanted success I had to learn how to forage for sales, or go hungry. I leaned into discomfort, and by year's end, after learning the basics, I earned nearly double my previous salary as a business reporter at Dunn and Bradstreet. Provision was there all along, but I never would have enjoyed it if I had not done what was necessary.

Instead of waiting for motivation, I encourage you to exercise discipline, which is the fruit of vision[2], then do the hard thing, and uncover the provision God has laid up for you. Birds don't wait to forage until they feel like it. They forage because that is how they access what God has already set aside. Success belongs not merely to the brilliant, but to the consistent doer of fundamentals. Faithfulness and consistency, more than excitement, will feed you for the long haul. Constant action is not a burden when it matches your design.

Amazon is a multi-trillion-dollar company by market valuation. They didn't discover oil or patent water. They sell everyday items very well.

They got there in part, through relentless daily improvements, tiny adjustments, continuous optimization, and refinement of thousands of inhouse micro-systems. Jeff Bezos reportedly said, "Our success at Amazon is a function of how many experiments we do per year, per month, per week, per day." That's what birds do instinctively, many small actions producing compounded results.

Consistency

Jesus chose sparrows for a reason. They are small, ordinary, and everywhere. And yet they never fail to find food. Why? Because they never stop foraging. Watch them sometime... They hop. Then they scratch the surface, maybe peck a bit, and sift through what they find. They are in constant search for food, but not out of anxiety or panic, it's just how they are wired.

The heart of Matthew 6 is that daily provision is guaranteed, but it is still up to the bird to move with its design and gather what it needs for itself and its family. Provision is set aside for the faithful gatherer, not for the doubter, the procrastinator, or the worrier, but for the one who moves with steady trust. A sparrow doesn't say, "I'm too tired today. What if there's no food?" It simply does what God wired it to do and always finds provision.

What defeats many people in their calling or business is not the size of the task, but the absence of consistent daily actions that produce reliable, predictable success. Birds understand by instinct if they keep moving every day, they eventually rise, not through frenzied action, not through fear, but through steady faithful alignment with their God given design and purpose. Do the small things daily, and the large things follow in due season.

Birds don't ask, "Where can I make the most money?" They live by a better question, "Where does my design meet provision?" That is the rhythm of the Kingdom. That is the gospel of the foraging bird.

Seven Summary Points to Remember

1. Provision is set aside in the lane your design was built for.
2. Provision hides from the fearful and is revealed to the expectant.
3. Provision is found near your faithfulness more than in distant lands.
4. Provision is revealed more by timing than by effort.
5. What you notice, may be a clue to what you were meant to forage for.
6. Direction is clarified more while moving, than while waiting.
7. Provision feeds you while you gather it.

Turn to Chapter Six to discover how to tap into abundant provision by cooperating with the 13 Laws of Foraging,

References: 1) 2 Corinthians 9:8 2) Proverbs 29:18

CHAPTER 6

TAPPING INTO ABUNDANT PROVISION

Thirteen Laws For Successful Foraging

"God doesn't withhold provision... He hides it in layers, and only design reveals which layer your provision is found in."

The inspiration for this book was what Jesus said in Matthew 6 about how God provides for birds, with the conclusion of the matter found in verse 33...

> "Seek first the kingdom of God and His righteousness, and all these things shall be added to you."

If you miss that point, you miss the most important part of His message. That is why I listed it as the first law.

1. THE LAW OF EARLY SEEKING *"They that seek Me early shall find Me*[1]*."* Long before the world stirs, the robin steps into a realm most creatures never witness. The sky is still ink black, and the horizon is barely discernible. Yet the robin is already up and at it. It's not agitated, uptight, or worried. It is not even in a hurry. The robin rises when God stirs it, its tiny feet pressing into dew laden grass. Each step it takes demonstrates a bond of trust in a supply it has not yet seen.

It's show time! It's the best part of the day for him. He rises aligned with design and purpose when God Himself stirs the gifts. If the robin rises too early, the provision remains unseen. Too late, and the provision goes to another. But in that precise moment, when night is about to tumble off the horizon and morning is about to rise, provision and purpose, design, and instinct, meet in perfect harmony.

But before he forages, he sings. The robin will spend 30 – 60 minutes in song to "warm up" his internal systems, establish boundaries, announce intentions, and listen for signals that indicate where food is, such as the movement of an earthworm working its way to the surface.

Hosea 2:18 says that God will make a covenant for the birds of the air and Psalm 150:6 says, "Let everything that has breath praise the Lord." I don't know the details of God's covenant with birds, but I do know that they have breath and I believe that some of their singing is them giving joyful expression, that glorifies the One they're in covenant with.

God's lesson is simple, acknowledge the Source
before seeking the supply.

When you begin your day with the Lord, you discover He's been getting things in place for you even while you slept. Your role is to seek Him first. In business and in life, the early seeker is not merely the one who rises early...

It's the one who listens before labor.

Before checking your inbox, your notifications, even before your calendar, before your mind fills with noise, seek the whisper. Seek alignment. Seek the Lord. When you do, opportunities rise toward you like worms ascending to meet the robin's faith-filled expectation.

When Matthew 6:33 says, "Seek first the kingdom of God and His righteousness, and all these things will be added to you", for me, that was more like a formula or inspirational slogan, than a guide for successful living. For most of my Christian walk, it meant I would maybe read a bible verse and say a short prayer, then get on with my day. Five minutes max.

Then, in 1994 when a business crisis came my way, I found out that the purpose of seeking God was to actually find Him, not just check a box.

What a concept! So, I decided to spend open-ended time in the morning enveloped in God's Word until His presence became real to me. I don't mean anything mystical here. I would press into His Word until it came alive on the inside of me. Sometimes that was right away. Sometimes longer. Once His Word was speaking to me, I stayed with it until that lifted. It was never less than an hour, and usually around three hours, sometimes five hours.

I was actually working less than normal but the strangest thing began to happen. My publisher called out of the blue and had me do three books in a row with good royalty advances. The INSP television network invited me to do an informercial for one of my teaching series. My phone started to ring with opportunities I didn't know existed and they all provided well for me.

I experienced what Jesus meant when He said, "And all these things will be ADDED to you." Instead of trying to be the rainmaker and do all the adding to my supply, I became the "rain catcher", following the cloud of God's presence and catching the provision He had abundantly stored up for me.

Practical Tip

One way to keep your mind free from activity and updates first thing in the morning is to close out the previous day with a review and a plan for tomorrow. That way, when you rise, you already know nothing pressing will be lost if it waits until the workday begins.

The best business advice I can give you is simply this... Pursue God. Marinate your mind in His Word. Let the Word speak. Ask the Holy Spirit to teach you. Wait on Him. Listen. Write down what comes to you, then act on it!

2. THE LAW OF TARGET-RICH PATCHES *"He makes me lie down in green pastures.*[3]*"* After having laid out the foundation of The Law of Early Seeking, let me take you over to a lush green pasture and learn from David, the one whom Scripture calls, a man after God's own heart[2] talked about in Psalm 23. In the previous verse David starts off the Psalm with an incredibly powerful statement, often quoted, but rarely understood. It reads,

"The Lord is my Shepherd; **I shall not want**."

Most people consider these words, comforting, that somehow God will eventually come through, if not in this lifetime, then certainly in the next. But that is not the point.

This statement is not a future hope... It's a present reality. Ignore it at your own loss. With God, lack is impossible. You can no more threaten God's ability to provide abundantly than you can drain the ocean with a straw. When David says, "I shall not want", that was a declaration of reality, making lack for him, (as far as he was concerned), an impossibility.

The reason he knew that lack was not his portion was because the LORD Himself was his shepherd, leading him in the way he should go. The shepherd's responsibility is not merely to keep the sheep alive. A good shepherd leads them to abundant green pastures and fresh water.

Birds do not store up treasure, but they are expert economists. They don't waste time or energy working barren ground. Neither should you. A finch surveys the land before setting its feet on it. A heron takes up its post in shallow water where it knows fish gather. Have you ever seen a swallow flying through a meadow? It goes where the gnats are abundant. Birds instinctively know abundance is not everywhere, but they know it's definitely somewhere, and they go there!

When you see a warbler flitting through the branches, it's not wasting time in aimless wandering. It's moving with focused intention until it finds what every forest forager knows to look for, a target rich patch. The warbler, like any savvy person, knows not to linger where the ROI is low. It's looking for concentrations of food, where provision comes in clusters and renews itself.

I have been in the Ecuadorian rainforest, off the beaten trail and I experienced what birds already know; that life pools in pockets, provision forms in predictable zones, and blessing gathers in patterns of:

- Design (nectar gathers in specific flower shapes)
- Timing (worms surface after the rain)
- Rhythm (forage, rest, and return)
- Relationship (flocking birds find food faster)
- Attention (seeing what matters)
- Obedience (staying true to their design)

Birds understand all this and simply repeat, day after day, what works.

God's Lesson: God often hides abundance in concentrated places. That's why people join mastermind groups, attend trade shows, join clubs, and go to conferences and seminars. These environments often concentrate abundance in relationships, ideas, markets, and partnerships, places where harvest is already prepared.

Wisdom is not about beating your brains out and working hard everywhere. It is about working faithfully where concentrated harvest is possible. Birds don't pray for food to land in their nest. They go where God has already placed it.

Application: Success comes faster when you operate in target rich environments. Who are the prospects that are already hungry? Who are the prospects already looking for what you have? Where are the arenas where your gifts naturally multiply? In your work, find the target rich patches, the markets, relationships, or ideas where response is highest, and resistance is lowest. Spend your effort there. The Lord of the harvest is also the Lord of the habitat.

3. THE LAW OF GIVING UP DENSITY "*Let us lay aside every weight.*[4]..." The fox sparrow is an enterprising little bird that spends much of its time deep in the underbrush, rummaging through leaf litter in search of insects. Sometimes the leaf debris looks promising, and it can detect the faintest rustle of hidden movement.

It forages by scratching to stir things up, then listening for motion, then scratching again, hoping to find insects scurrying for cover. But at times there is little response, or worse, nothing but silence. The patch that once served it, has gone quiet because the insects have moved on. What formerly promised provision is now empty ground.

It has encountered diminishing returns, but instead of drowning in sorrow, the sparrow does what many struggle to do. It moves on. It is a simple, calculated, almost emotionless decision, not made in frustration or panic, but in economic wisdom.

Birds live by a principal biologists call "giving up density". They're not interested in throwing good money after bad. If their time investment no longer yields sufficient ROI, they don't get nostalgic about it. They shake off the unproductive patch and look for better ground. Simply put, when the density of reward drops below a profitable threshold, they stop. What is that threshold for you?

God's Lesson: Fields or streams of provision have a shelf life. Your job is to shift when that season ends instead of demanding it stay the same. Solomon instructed us in Ecclesiastes 3:1, "To everything there is a season, a time for every purpose under heaven." When one season of provision ends, another is coming. It will be different, but God will not abandon you.

Wisdom is the courage to release what is no longer fruitful, whether habits, strategies, relationships, or assignments, so you can enter fields and seasons God has freshly prepared. Do not linger in yesterday's blessing as though you will never have another. What once was a place of provision can become a place of famine if you do not move when the season changes.

4. THE LAW OF QUIET FOOTING *"In quietness and confidence shall be your strength.*[5]*"* The heron is a master of quiet footing, the art of moving so calmly, so patiently, so quietly, that it could slip past a motion detector unnoticed. The heron knows even the smallest ripple carries meaning and, to the discerning eye, reveals secrets. If the heron made a ruckus upon landing, or was careless with its footing, the fish would be gone in a flash. Therein is the heron's secret knowledge...

Provision flees commotion and
opportunity withdraws from chaos.

God's Lesson: For the heron, stillness is not passivity. It is not hesitation, fear, or uncertainty. Stillness is strength. Like the heron, the quiet heart hears subtle cues others miss. When you walk softly in peace, you notice doors God opens that you did not even know to look for. When your footing is quiet, discernment sharpens, and God's timing becomes clear.

Anxiety makes noise that pushes opportunity away, while wisdom speaks softly and attracts it. Slow your internal pace. Move with intention. Let peace be the platform from which you survey the room and perceive opportunity. The calm leader sees what anxious leaders trample. The quiet seeker finds what noise chases away.

5. THE LAW OF PATCH RENEWAL *"Behold, I am doing a new thing... shall you not perceive it?*[6]*"* As summer begins to loosen its grip and autumn clears its throat in preparation for change, the goldfinch gathers seeds from thistles and coneflowers. But the goldfinch does not merely revisit the same feeding ground every day. It tracks the cycle of renewal. It knows which areas replenish quickly and which operate on a slower cycle. It harvests what it can from a patch, then moves on, but not forever. It knows that its favorite fields renew, regrow, and repopulate with supply.

A few weeks later when sunlight and warmth have ripened more of the field, and wind or rain has softened or opened new seed heads, the goldfinch returns with expectancy. It knows the law of patch renewal. The patch that was bare weeks ago is once again brimming with provision.

God's Lesson: God is the initiator of renewal. "He restores my soul.[7]" He builds renewal into every life. When life looks depleted and barren, renewal is not far away. Renewal cannot come until the old has passed. Do not get stuck grieving the barren season. It may simply be the stage that precedes renewal. What looks empty to you may simply be a season change where abundance is gathering beneath the surface.

6. THE LAW OF WEATHER WINDOWS *"To everything there is a season, and a time to every purpose under heaven.[8]"* Looking overhead recently, I saw a flock of sandhill cranes drifting by. Change was in the air, and they knew it. A subtle shift in wind direction, a lowering of barometric pressure, and they instinctively recognized that a narrow weather window, unseen and undetected by most people, had opened. Florida was nice, but it was time to head back north. Migration season was beginning.

Cranes don't wait until the mood strikes them. They don't choose their moment based on preference. They wait for atmospheric conditions that maximize lift, minimize drag, and transport them hundreds of miles with minimal effort. The invisible forces they recognize will carry them. It's like catching a northbound train. You go when the train is leaving, not when you feel like it.

Timing is everything. The law of weather windows teaches that success does not always go to the strongest[9]. It often goes to the best timed. Provision is not only the result of effort, as important as effort is. It is also the fruit of alignment with God's timing. Provision follows perception. Ask God to reveal not just the task, but the timing. Timing is God's way of giving Divine leverage.

7. THE LAW OF INCREMENTAL ADVANCEMENT *"Here a little, there a little.*[10]" The woodpecker knows that provision is rarely found in large quantities. Instead, it is discovered through steady, systematic advancement. It does not matter how large the tree is. The woodpecker knows there is no need to rush.

If it maintains and trusts its process of small advancements and consistent, faithful effort, it will be well fed along the way. A small gain here, a larva there, and before you know it, it has a full belly, a well-nourished nest, and a life of worry-free abundance. For the woodpecker, it was never about winning the lottery and finding a barrel full of larvae. It is about the steady uncovering of unseen abundance that has been there all along, just beneath the surface.

God's Lesson: God often leads through gradual steps, not giant leaps. The overnight success did not happen overnight. It was the result of faithful work, many tiny course corrections, usually worked out in obscurity, until the moment of breakthrough. Proverbs 13:11 says,

> "Whoever gathers money little by little, makes it grow."

Jesus likened the growth of the kingdom of God to the growth pattern of a seed that gets planted, watered, and grows steadily.

8. THE LAW OF MIXED FLOCKS *"Two are better than one... for they have a good reward for their labor.*[11]" An interesting phenomenon occurs in the deep woods of the Northeast United States and Canada. Various species like chickadees, titmice, nuthatches, warblers, and woodpeckers, which normally stay in their own clique, begin traveling together, forming a mixed flock of living synergy.

Every bird brings something different to the party. It is a dream team, each gift benefiting the others while doing what comes natural to them. As a result, danger is averted faster, food is found quicker and in greater abundance, energy is conserved, and survival rates skyrocket! Better yet, no bird has to deny its identity. There is no pressure to be like the other guy. It is a strategic community that multiplies return on energy through shared presence.

God's Lesson: God designed increase to flow through collaboration, not isolation. Your gifts sharpen others. Their gifts can cover your lack. What you cannot see, someone else can. What you cannot reach, someone else can reach with ease.

Application: In business and life, your mixed flock is your strategic circle, mentors, peers, collaborators, partners, intercessors, and advisors. Do not always forage alone. Build alliances with people who complement your strengths and compensate for blind spots.

9. THE LAW OF ENERGY CONSERVATION *"My yoke is easy, and My burden is light.*[12]" Smaller birds exhaust themselves flying from tree to tree, while the hawk has learned to rise on borrowed strength. This is not laziness. It is mastery. Raptors understand what all of us would benefit from knowing:

Wasted energy is stolen opportunity.

The hawk observes the skies and watches other birds, looking for unseen currents and rising temps that will give lift. When its wingtip senses warmer air on one side, it tilts its body and, with ease, slips into the updraft, allowing God's natural forces to carry it higher.

God's Lesson: God designed you to operate in grace, not grind. Hebrews 4 tells us there is a rest for the people of God, and we are to be diligent to enter that rest. This is not a call to lie in a hammock and count clouds. It's a promise that when you move in alignment with the wind of God, in His timing, following His leading, and leaning on His wisdom, tasks become lighter and victory more certain. Strength multiplies when you stop striving in your own power and learn to trust God and ride on His strength.

10. THE LAW OF OPPORTUNITY WAVES *"To everything there is a season, a time for every purpose under heaven:*[13]" I lived many years on the West Coast of British Columbia and spent time walking the rugged beaches of the Pacific facing side of Vancouver Island. As a teenager, I canoed the fjords of Princess Louisa Inlet, where it seemed that oysters were more numerous than rocks.

In that region there is a bird known as the black oystercatcher, whose mission in life seems to be standing on wave drenched rocks waiting for the tide to shift. The cool Pacific waves crash upward and expose clinging mussels and limpets. In that brief moment, their grip loosens and their guard drops, just what the black oystercatcher is waiting for. Their shells open slightly, as if to catch a breath, and in that instant, it darts forward, plunges its chisel like beak into the opening, and pulls. One well timed strike. One strong pull. One well deserved victory.

If it misses that moment and does not respond in time, it does not panic. It knows in practice, what Solomon described in Ecclesiastes 1:9, "What has been, will be again, what has been done, will be done again." It knows another wave is coming. Opportunity is rhythmic. Some might even say seasonal. That means it's predictable for the one who understands the pattern. Study the rhythm of your industry. Identify the moments when clients are most receptive, or market conditions favor your offer. Success comes to those prepared to strike when the opportunity crests.

11. THE LAW OF FORAGING ORDER *"Let all things be done decently and in order.*[14]*"* There is a species of bird called the cedar waxwing. What is striking about the way it approaches the tree is the orderliness of its feeding. It forages in a disciplined pattern, sweeping the tree from top to bottom, then branch to branch, ensuring nothing is wasted. If you watch shorebirds, you will notice they probe the sand in structured grids. Sparrows work patches of grass in widening spirals.

Birds know what we could all benefit from: that disorder eats time, burns energy, and makes it easy to skip over provision without realizing it. A structured approach yields more with less effort. Simply put, when life is orderly, abundance multiplies.

God's Lesson: God blesses order. That doesn't require perfection, but wise structure brings increase. Disorder drains resources, while order gathers them. Random effort produces random results. If you want a predictable, repeatable harvest, adopt an orderly approach to life and business.

12. THE LAW OF HIDDEN ABUNDANCE *"The kingdom of heaven is like treasure hidden in a field.*[15]*"* The key word here may be, "hidden". The treasure is in the field, but you have to find it. Deep in the forest, scratching through tangled fallen branches, wet leaves, and overgrown ferns, you find the winter wren. That little wren will disappear beneath a rotting redwood tree that fell in a storm a year ago, then burst out later with excitement, as if to say, "Look what I got!" It carries a spider no larger bird could ever reach. The wren thrives not because it has more opportunities or is better equipped, but because it is willing to forage where others refuse to go.

Hidden treasure is the reward of the curious, the attentive, the persistent, the risk takers, and those not quick to quit. The richest blessings are often buried, waiting for the one willing to buy the whole field, not just pick up what lies on the surface.

Hidden abundance requires you to seek, not skim. It trains you to see what God has set aside for you in places others ignore.

13. THE LAW OF THE FOCUSED FEASTS *"If your eye is single, your whole body will be full of light.*[16] There is a reason they call this next bird a kingfisher. The kingfisher knows the river teems with life, but it's not waiting for just any fish to pass. It's looking for one good fish – the one it wants. Then it happens. Without hesitation, the kingfisher becomes a javelin of blue lightning with bullet-like efficiency aimed at a single target. Its body pierces the water with barely a splash, eyes locked on the prize.

When the kingfisher erupts back into the air, water shedding off its sleek body, it carries in its bill the object of its focus, the prize it sought, dinner for itself and its mate as the sun drops. This is the focused feast, the product of concentration and disciplined attention. Other birds along the river's edge scatter attention across many opportunities, but the kingfisher commits to one target, one well timed moment, one decisive strike. Because of that, its success rate is off the charts.

God multiplies the life of the focused heart.

Instability in life doesn't come from the storm, it comes from split attention. Think of it this way. When your vision is divided, your provision is diluted. When your attention is pulled in many directions, opportunities blur. But when your eye is single, focused on God's leading and assignment, vision sharpens, timing aligns, and breakthrough becomes predictable and precise.

Commit to one target at a time. Choose your river. Focus intently. Strike with precision. Your harvest will increase in proportion to your focus.

Turn to Chapter 7 and discover the secret ritual birds practice that you can use to elevate your game.

References: 1) Proverbs 8:17 2) 1 Samuel 13:14. 3) Psalm 23:2 4) Hebrews 12:1 5) Isaiah 30:15 6) Isaiah 43:19 7) Psalm 23:3 8) Ecclesiastes 3:1 9) Ecclesiastes 9:1 10) Isaiah 28:10 11) Ecclesiastes 4:9 12) Matthew 11:30 13) Ecclesiastes 3:1 14) 1 Corinthians 14:40 15) Matthew 13:44 16) Matthew 6:22

CHAPTER 7

THE SECRET SURVIVAL RITUAL

How Preening Elevates Your Game

"Excellence is the residue of relentless refinement."

For as long as man has been on this planet, he has been captivated and inspired by birds in ways no other creature on earth can do. Why birds and not fish? Why birds and not four-footed animals? Because birds can fly! And the ability, by choice and without effort, to catch the unseen wind and fly in any direction, or simply soar from on high and enjoy the sights, gives them what everyone wants deep down inside...

FREEDOM

Hence the title of this book. Flight is liberating in ways that walking, running, or swimming are not. Flight gives you options. With the ability to fly, you can travel faster, farther, and freer than any other creature. We get caught up in the wonder of flying and imagine the freedom it would give us if we could, like a bird, take flight. We picture it the way someone imagines spending lottery winnings. A pleasant dream perhaps, but reality is different. So it is with birds.

Their ability to fly effortlessly and beautifully depends on something we tend to pay little attention to. Preening... It's the act of self-maintenance that preserves their ability to fly. Depending on the species, on any given day a bird will spend anywhere from two to ten times as much time preparing to fly as actually flying.

If you want to be free as a bird, to soar to great heights or simply fly above the conflicts below, you're going to need to preen. There is no getting around it. Your natural giftings (your wings) will only take you so far. If you want to survive for the long haul and thrive in any environment, you will need to preen daily. That means spending more time developing and honing your craft than showcasing it to others.

Preening is the difference between rising and falling, between surviving a challenge or being ravaged by it, between readiness and destruction. It's the daily unglamorous work of restoring alignment, removing what drains you, and reinforcing what makes your life and work effortless under pressure. How and whether you choose to preen will determine the altitude of your destiny.

There are four big reasons birds preen. Here they are...

I) Structure and Order (Feather Alignment)
Action: If a bird's feathers are out of alignment, it hinders its ability to fly and the freedom that brings. To maintain its flying ability at a high level, it realigns feather barbs and barbules, so they interlock correctly. That process creates smoother airflow, maximizes lift, minimizes drag, and prevents turbulence. Feathers are the structures that make flight possible. For optimal lift and smoother flight, they must be aligned with each other, not in conflict.

When it comes to alignment, I think of three alignments that determine how high you rise, how far you go, and how fast you get there.

1. Alignment with the unseen power of God. When birds fly, they trust in what they cannot see to get them to where they want to go. They don't burn energy flying into the wind. They align with it to rise and travel further in less time. For you and me, that means aligning with God's Word and being led and carried by His Spirit. Bring your motives, goals, and actions into alignment with God's will and His ways for maximum success.

2. Alignment with others: When key relationships are not aligned, it creates tension that holds you back. Before taking on any project, straighten out relational alignment issues. Jesus said in Matthew 5:23-24

> "Therefore, if you bring your gift to the altar, and there remember that your brother has something against you, leave your gift there before the altar, and go your way. *First be reconciled to your brother*, and then come and offer your gift."

3. Alignment with resources: Don't attempt to climb Mt. Everest in shorts and a T-shirt. As much as possible find the right tools and training for the task at hand. Using the wrong tool, or inadequate skills for the job, creates friction and slows you down.

II) Removing Contamination (Feather Cleanliness)
Action: Whether foraging for food on the ground or lounging in their nest, birds can get dirty. God made them to want to be clean, so they preen to remove dust, dirt, parasites, debris, and even salt. This reduces weight, prevents disease, keeps them well insulated, and maintains the function of their feathers.

Application: One of the greatest hindrances to gaining elevation in life is the contamination we pick up in our thoughts. Negative, depressing, fear based, toxic input will hold you down. The destructive thoughts we give space to are parasitic in nature because they drain vitality and suck the life out of you. They will not leave on their own.

Solomon said, "As a man thinks, so is he," If you change your thoughts (INPUT), you will change your life. If you find your mind going down a dark path, it's virtually impossible to simply stop thinking about it. You have to replace it with another line of thought, choosing a different topic. In other words, fresh input.

Allow me to recommend some fresh input that has been a strength to me from God's Word... Psalm 34:10 promises,

> "But those who seek the Lord shall not lack any good thing."

Psalm 84:11 adds,

> "No good thing will He withhold from those who walk uprightly."

I don't know about you, but that's the kind of input I want... the promises of God, found in His Word to anyone who seeks the Lord and walks uprightly. *Let's go!*

III) Micro Corrections (Feather Repair)
Action: Birds use their feathers every day, and as a result, there is always something that needs fixing. They are in constant repair mode, taking care of bent or separated barbs. These are not major overhauls, but small corrections that prevent compounding damage, avoid major impairment, and keep flight smooth and aerodynamically sound.

Application: The Bible says it's the little foxes that spoil the vine[3], and tiny flies that ruin expensive perfume[4]. Paul put it another way, "A little leaven leavens the whole lump.[5]" Ask yourself, what poor habits are trying to creep into your life? Do not let them gain a stronghold. Where have you slightly compromised your integrity? Make it right. Where are your motives not right? Be honest with yourself and do the right things for the right reasons. These small adjustments protect you when bigger tests come. A series of small compromises becomes a habit that can open the door to larger failure.

IV) Identity (Fidelity to Design)
Action: The variation in feather design, color, and function in the bird world is astonishing. Birds carefully maintain feathers specific to their

species and make no attempt to be like another species. Consider the puffin found along the North Atlantic coast. This bird can fly around sixty miles per hour, but unlike most birds, it can also fly underwater at up to ten miles per hour and dive to depths of two hundred feet. No osprey or pelican can do that, nor do they try.

Every bird species sticks with its design. You do not see robins diving for fish or puffins hunting worms. When birds preen, they don't adjust their feathers to imitate another species. They preen to maximize the design God gave them.

Application: Preening is largely about honing your skills to become the best version of you to glorify God in all you do. Honor your unique calling, disposition, and assignment. Preening is obedience to design.

It is not about conforming to something God never wired you for. Ask yourself, what does it mean today, to be faithful to your design? Stick with what you are best suited for, regardless of how much money, fame, or success others who are wired differently than you, pursue. People often look at successful individuals and underestimate what it took for that success to manifest.

Excellence is not a natural birthright.
It's the residue of relentless refinement.

Skill in any endeavor is the product of disciplined care and attention to the traits required for success. If you want to see the importance of preening in nature relative to a high calling in God, watch the eagle. When an eagle preens, it is a matter of survival. It passes its golden beak along every feather shaft, aligning, cleaning, and oiling them. It tends its wings like a Marine tends his rifle before battle.

Eagle level assignment requires eagle level maintenance.

The eagle preens because its mission and design require strength and structural integrity. So does yours. Companies that preen, thrive, because their systems stay clean, their teams stay trained, and their culture stays healthy. Companies that neglect maintenance fall apart from within, often while still projecting strength outwardly.

I have hunted in the rugged mountains of British Columbia, slept beneath the Milky Way, and watched the sunrise spill through the first crack in the surrounding peaks. If you look closely, you might see an eagle already perched on a ledge overlooking the alpine meadow below. As the sun rises and the Indian Paintbrush and Avalanche Lilies catch the first rays and open their splendor, the earth welcomes the warmth and releases rising thermals back to the heavens.

The eagle knows the rhythm of the unfolding day. He smells the fragrance of alpine flowers drifting upward. His eyes search for prey. He was born for this moment, and he knows it. Like an astronaut running through a final pre-launch checklist, he checks each feather shaft, sensing any misalignment that could throw off his dive, detecting micro damage that could foil success. He's not in a hurry, but he's not casual either. He is precise. Calculated. Determined. His nature urges him to launch, but he waits.

He will not bend to desire
until discipline has completed its work.

He oils his primary feathers that cut into the wind, his secondary feathers that shape lift, even the hidden feathers that seal gaps. All are important and must be attended to before yielding to the exhilaration that awaits when he spreads his wings and steps into what he was created to do.

He sees a rabbit scurrying below on the alpine floor miles away, heading in his direction. He keeps preening and preparing. His mate and chicks depend on his success. He will not let haste or fear drive him. Seconds become minutes. Minutes feel like an eternity to the casual observer, but the eagle knows what matters.

When his preening ritual is complete, he scans the valley once more. A warm thermal rises to his perch. He steps into the abyss with total confidence. With one powerful downward stroke he commits to the air and is lifted high above the ledge. He glides effortlessly toward his prey, his plumage glowing in the fiery radiance of the morning sun.

The eagle flies well because he prepared
before he flew. Your life is no different.

It is hard to soar without renewal or to lead when things are not properly aligned. You cannot build a consistent pattern of success without preening – that deliberate attention to self-improvement, enabled by the grace of God and ignited by the love of God shed abroad in your heart[6]. Allow that love for God and for people to grow deep within you, and the discipline to preen will come so naturally it will scarcely feel like effort.

Your wings, your mind, will, emotions, spirit, character, skills, systems, and relationships must all be maintained. The Holy Spirit stands ready with fresh oil to empower you, Scripture to lead you into truth, and wisdom to guide you.

If you truly want the secret of worry-free living in God's abundance, whether retired, employed, or running a business, you must take preening (and training) seriously. It will lead you to heights you never imagined.

Those who renew deeply, rise highest.

And somewhere beneath your own cliff of decision, a world waits, not only for your ideas, products, sermons, or strategies, but for the inspiration of a life that truly soars with ease.

So before you leap into the next demand, the next opportunity, the next battle, or the next stage of your calling…

Preen.

Once you've preened, you're ready to soar. Chapter 8 invites you to discover the secret of effortless flight.

References: 1) Proverbs 23:7 2) Matthew 12:34 3) Song of Solomon 2:15 4) Ecclesiastes 10:1 5) Galatians 5:9 6) Romans 5:5

CHAPTER 8

THE SECRET OF EFFORTLESS FLIGHT

The Law of Lift Over Drag

"We rise in life by aligning and cooperating with God's laws of lift, not by mere exhausting stress and strain."

Do you remember the first time you felt the sky?

For me, it wasn't up in the clouds. It was in the backseat of a 1957 Chevrolet Bel Air on a summer day when I was riding in the back with the window down. We weren't traveling fast, just driving in town, but curiosity tugged on my imagination as I put my hand out the window.

What a feeling! As the wind coursed through my fingers at 30 mph, I tilted my hand upward, and my whole hand lifted. The same would happen in reverse if I pointed down. My hand was flying, and whatever direction I pointed it, the wind would accelerate it in that direction. But imagine with me for a moment if your life was tied to the air more than to the land. What if your body was always negotiating with gravity, air density, turbulence, updrafts, downdrafts, crosswinds, and unseen currents? Not just when you stick your hand out the window of a fast-moving car or facing off against a hurricane.

What if it was a way of life for you, where every stroke of your wing was a negotiation with a force you could not see? Unlike me when I didn't know better, birds understand wind and its currents. They are not victims of the storm. They know how to glide, how to soar, and how to dance on top of unseen currents as if the wind itself were their dance partner.

The wind is much bigger than any bird. They know not to fight it.

Instead, they have learned to partner with it. They know that lift must exceed drag or they will be stuck on the ground and vulnerable to attack. You can flap your wings until your muscles burn and your feathers wear out, but if the forces pulling you down are stronger than those lifting you up and forward, you will remain grounded.

Birds have this figured out, and they master it. People on the other hand, have not fully grasped the implications and application to life, so they ignore what they do not understand. This chapter is about the four invisible forces that influence how high you rise in life. It's about how birds have mastered those forces, and what anyone in business, ministry, marriage, or a calling of some kind must do if they ever hope to ascend to the pinnacle of what God created them to do.

It's about mastering the four invisible forces so you can rise to the fullness of God's plan for your life. It is about gaining lift and eliminating drag in life, which makes the difference between a life of striving filled with anxious toil, and a nearly effortless ascent to heights you never dreamed possible.

The Four Great Forces and the Law of Alignment

Every bird must master these four laws that govern all flight...

1. Lift: The upward force that counters gravity.
2. Drag: The backward force that resists motion.
3. Thrust: The forward push generated by flapping wings.
4. Gravity: The downward pull on the body of the bird.

Lift is generated by the shape of the wing, curved on top, forcing air to move farther in the same amount of time, creating a pressure difference that pulls the wing upward. Drag comes from anything that catches or redirects airflow like a damaged feather, bad angles, excess weight, or misaligned movements. Thrust and weight require no explanation. Lift and drag are almost imperceptible, but they decide the success or failure of any flight attempt.

I remember the first time I ever flew. It was in a 1970 Toyota, my mother's car, which I had borrowed at age seventeen to travel from British Columbia across the Continental Divide to Calgary, Alberta with a friend. On the 600-mile return trip to the West Coast, I took over driving to let him sleep. It was around 6:30 AM and we were just beginning to ascend through the foothills toward the Rockies.

I was in a hurry to get home, so I was a little aggressive with my speed as we climbed the mountain range. Eventually I became tired and reclined my seat to drive more comfortably, and quite predictably I fell asleep and crossed into the oncoming lane of the Trans Canada Highway.

Fortunately, there was no one coming in that lane, and as the wheels hit the gravel shoulder on the opposite side of the road, I awoke just as we became airborne. The RCMP later estimated my speed as the car headed into open air at 85 mph. As I surveyed the new terrain and marveled at the treetops passing by on my way down the mountain, still airborne, I remember thinking, "This is the first time I've ever flown."

I was experiencing the law of thrust. Moments later, the law of gravity, the law of drag, and the necessary but, not in play, law of lift, all took part as the car hit the first boulder and then bounced end over end down the mountainside. We had no seatbelts on and were like dice in a can being tossed around the cabin.

My friend Dale had a couple of facial cuts requiring stitches, but I had not a scratch or bruise on my body. We hiked back up the mountain and hitchhiked roughly eighteen miles east to the nearest town of Revelstoke. After Dale got stitched up and we filed the accident report, we caught a Greyhound bus to the West Coast.

The bus did not have two seats together when we got on, so we sat where we could. The gentleman beside me listened to my story and told me that God must have a plan for my life. Although I was instantly repulsed by religion, I was very attracted to the idea that God might want to "hire" me. It was that day that the idea of destiny awoke in me, and I had to find it. A few months later I did. But I digress.

Birds are not confused by the four laws of flight. They know they will rise when they minimize drag, maximize lift, and generate enough thrust to get moving while keeping their weight within the limits dictated by their design. They know the more they reduce drag, the less thrust they require to get airborne.

Their goal is not to learn how to flap harder any more than our goal should be to work harder. No. Their goal is to create or cooperate with conditions where floating becomes almost effortless. We tend to think greater effort is always the answer. Just try harder! We work longer, push harder, and demand more of ourselves. But birds know effort alone is not the answer. We forget what I call the God Factor.

Jesus said our Heavenly Father feeds the birds. They seem to know that, and operate on a level of faith and trust that we would do well to learn from. We rise in life by aligning and cooperating with God's laws of lift, not by exhausting stress and strain. Gaining lift is not so much a reward for hard work as it is the result of cooperating with your design in harmony with the laws of God. In Biblical terms, drag is the weight of sin that so easily ensnares us, which we are told to lay aside[1]. Lift is the wind of the Spirit beneath the wings of the one who waits on the Lord[2].

One of the more amazing illustrations in the bird world of a creature that has mastered the laws governing flight is the Wandering Albatross. With wings spanning up to twelve feet, it spends most of its life gliding effortlessly over the ocean. It will spend over a year at sea, resting and feeding on waves, then rising to soar again, sometimes on autopilot mode, with half its brain sleeping while the other half navigates the flight. It will not set foot on solid ground for over a year, and in that time will travel some 120,000 miles, staying aloft for days at a time, barely flapping its wings. What looks like free energy is really pure physics exquisitely exploited.

This is not a creature with massive strength. He has learned the secrets of the wind, partnering with it, preferring its company over what he finds on land. The exception is mating season, when he will fly back to the rugged coast of the southern end of the South Island of New Zealand and wait for his partner to return from her epic journey so they can mate and have chicks. They do this every year, remaining loyal to each other during their long separation.

While sailing over the Southern Ocean, they practice something called "dynamic soaring". When flying a few feet above the ocean surface, the wind is very slow due to friction, but higher up, the wind speed is faster and smoother. The albatross uses these different wind speeds to extract power without flapping its wings. In essence, it is borrowing energy from the difference in wind speeds, converting that difference into forward motion. Pretty ingenious, really.

In Scripture, the Holy Spirit is described or compared to the wind of God[3], something you can detect but cannot see. What if you could detect the Spirit and ride on His strength? Most people give that idea no serious consideration, choosing instead to flap harder and try to make it work. Not even Jesus did that. He said in John 5:19,

> "My Father has been working until now, and I have been working... Most assuredly, the Son can do nothing of Himself, but what He sees the Father do, for whatever He does, the Son also does in like manner."

Jesus only worked where He saw His Father working.

He goes on to say in John 5:30,

> "I can of Myself do nothing... because I do not seek My own will but the will of the Father who sent Me."

Jesus lived His life in total submission to the will of the Father, which allowed Him to do greater works that we may marvel[4]. I believe God spreads His provision liberally, but if you want to enter the realm of greater works or greater success, you will need to sense where God is working and join Him there.

I don't mean that if you hear there is revival in China you must rush to join Him there. It's more like this... Where is He working in your heart? What is He stirring within you? Have you ever felt God tugging on your heart to do something, or go in a specific direction? Maybe you went, or maybe you did not. But if you go in the direction He is leading, you will do greater works than if you don't. That does not mean there will be no resistance. The religious folks resisted Jesus and sought to kill Him because He healed on the Sabbath.

If you don't know where God is working in your heart, that is a cue to pursue Him. Marinate your mind in His Word. Make it your goal to dwell in the secret place of the Most High and abide under the shadow of the Almighty[5]. For me that means setting aside open-ended time, quieting my mind, and listening. That may be walking in the woods or sitting on the sofa in silence, trusting that when He, the Spirit of truth, has come, He will guide you into all truth[6].

The albatross knows how to angle his body and let lift do what frantic flapping never could. It has learned how to align with God's laws so it can cross oceans on the power of currents it did not create. If you want to gain altitude in your life, better relationships, more effective ministry, work, and business success, think in terms of tuning in to what God is saying, and following that instead of doubling down on your effort.

The world is full of unseen channels of opportunity that may look like perfect timing, great favor, and God inspired ideas, all in place to take you further than hard work ever could. Ask the Father if He is inviting you into any of them. If you sense His pleasure in it, then your job is to say yes, shape your wings to catch the wind, and take the leap, trusting the wind to do most of the work.

To apply the albatross principle to business, find a market segment or avatar with whom your message resonates, that your product uniquely satisfies, and for whom your timing is impeccable. Sales will come naturally. Word of mouth spreads. Affiliates come to the table. Partnerships are formed. When you apply the albatross principle to business, you're no longer fighting the wind. You're riding with it and harnessing its power.

The albatross taps into the free energy of wind to maximize longevity, staying out at sea for a year at a time, but the Red-Tailed Hawk is more focused on altitude, riding the thermals of destiny. On warm days, the sun heats the earth unevenly depending on ground cover. Some patches of land generate heat faster than others and warmer air begins to rise in invisible columns called thermals.

When you and I survey the landscape, we see nothing different, but to the Red-Tailed Hawk, there is opportunity to rise. I have seen it many times where I live, a hawk with wings spread wide, circling, rising higher and higher without flapping. It is not working harder. It is riding the escalator in the sky that no eyes can see. He has found a thermal. Isaiah 40:31 is a thermal verse.

> "Those who wait upon the Lord shall renew their strength;
> they shall mount up with wings like eagles."

To "wait" in that passage is not passivity or boredom. It is intentional positioning. For the hawk, it's waiting to feel the subtle surge of rising air. For you and me, it's listening prayer, heartfelt worship, and responsiveness to the slightest impression of the Spirit.

In that special time of waiting on the Lord, you can sense what might be called spiritual thermals, moments when you sense God's presence in a real and tangible way. You may be reading His Word and a passage jumps out that you have read a hundred times before, but suddenly it takes on special life and meaning for your life. When you rise in a spiritual thermal, you find yourself lifted into positions of influence and favor disproportionate to your exertion.

Back in 1985, I got caught up in an unexpected spiritual thermal. It was at a very low place in my life when my teenage marriage ended, my first-born child died, and I lost my two homes, vehicles, and everything but the clothes on my back. I was sleeping on someone else's couch and borrowing their car for transportation.

If ever I needed a lift, it was then. One morning I turned on the TV and saw The 700 Club program. I was not accustomed to watching it, but desperate for hope, I tuned in, albeit skeptically. As I stared at the TV watching the program, the scene changed and I saw myself being interviewed, with my name appearing below my image.

It freaked me out. I immediately got up and went for a walk in the West Coast rain that falls incessantly in February. I explained to God how bad things were down here and that I would never be invited on that program. He was not impressed.

So I asked if I would ever be established again, and I caught another thermal. He spoke 2 Chronicles 7:17-18 to me. I was not used to knowing His voice, but I ran to the car, got my Bible, and read it. Paraphrasing slightly, it said,

"As for you, if you will walk before me as David did, I will establish you."

In that moment, I caught a thermal of hope and my spirits lifted. Nearly sixteen years later, I was invited to be a guest on The 700 Club to discuss my book, ***Selling Among Wolves - Without Joining the Pack***. The interview aired four months later on the very day I was established again, as I closed on a home purchase and became a homeowner for the first time in nearly twenty years.

In life and business, thermals can take many forms. It may be a sudden "Aha" moment when you gain clarity. It could be unexpected favor or unplanned opportunity that knocks on your door. It could be a market trend perfectly timed for your assignment. It might be a subtle nudge to make a call that changes the course of your life, lifting you to heights you did not have the resources or connections to reach on your own.

Learn to recognize the thermals that lift and ride them higher instead of diffusing your energy in wasted effort that looks busy, even commendable, but is fruitless.

Catching the thermals of God's Spirit
makes gaining elevation – effortless.

You can accomplish in weeks or months what others cannot accomplish in years. This is the secret of the hawk and the eagle. Elevation is rarely the result of frantic flapping. It is far more likely and repeatable when you simply catch the rising current at the right time.

Turn to Chapter 9 to learn how to avoid the resistance that becomes sabotage!

References: 1) Hebrews 12:1 2) Isaiah 40:31 3) Acts 2:2, John 3:8, Genesis 1:2 4) John 5:20 5) Psalm 91:1 6) John 16:13

CHAPTER 9

WHEN RESISTANCE BECOMES SABOTAGE

The Heartbreak of Drag

"Breakthroughs follow simplification."

Anything that meets the wind the wrong way during flight is considered drag. It could be ruffled or bent feathers, a poorly executed wing angle, excess weight the bird may be carrying, like a fish it has just caught, or unnecessary motion that increases resistance. The more drag, the more energy it takes to maintain lift. Even parasites lodged in the feathers can increase the energy required to stay aloft and drain the bird of precious resources.

We've all felt drag in our lives. We may not have thought of it in those terms, but it's the emotional weight that makes the day feel heavy for no apparent reason. Some people call it "the blues," but it can also be fear, hesitancy, or poor self-esteem that makes simple tasks seem like mountains too big to climb. The drag I'm referring to is like sludge in the gears of your business and gum stuck to the bottom of your shoes, slowing you down.

It shows up under different names, usually with some justification. Fear shows up as second-guessing every decision for the umpteenth time, or replaying a bitter "someone done me wrong" song in your head. It has a voice that sounds just like you, whispering to your soul that you're not good enough, and never will be.

It creates insecurity that insists on constant reassurance and opens wounds that define how you see yourself and others. Every one of these (and a multitude of others) is like ruffled feathers catching the wind they were meant to miss, pulling you backward, slowing you down, urging you to stop flying and settle for low living.

Spiritual drag has its own subtlety. It shows up when casual compromise dulls your sensitivity to God, when obedience to His will becomes optional, when prayer reduces to "in case of emergency only," when influences hostile to true faith dictate your sense of right and wrong, and when you allow yourself to be conformed to this world instead of renewing your mind to think like God thinks, with full access to the mind of Christ[1].

Relational drag builds up when you stay in a relationship that is destructive to you, remain in parasitic one-sided relationships that only drain you, or try to hang with those going in a different direction than your calling. These and other similar relationships fit in the category of being unequally yoked and create constant internal resistance that slows you down.

Mental drag is easy to see. It looks like clutter, where your mind is full of fleeting thoughts about many things that have nothing to do with your life, your calling, or your well-being. It includes time-wasting distractions, overthinking simple things, indecision, and what I would call "social noise", the kind of things that show up in your social media feed that have no relevance or value to your life. A mind filled with random thoughts, unconnected to purpose or meaning, is like flying in turbulence of your own making, bouncing between stories, videos, and opinions that make merchandise of you.

Business drag looks like unclear messaging; shoddy or ineffective systems; customer journeys with so much friction in your sales process that people give up on the purchase; redundancy; and multiple layers of approval that suffocate innovation and slow things down to a grinding halt. Regardless of which kind of drag you're dealing with; they all have the same effect: they rob you of energy and motivation and reduce your altitude. They make you question your calling. Business becomes burdensome. Ministry seems obligatory rather than rewarding. Marriage loses its luster. Prayer feels pointless.

Birds treat drag as an emergency, but people often treat it as part of their identity. But here's what must be caught: just like one loose feather can compromise an entire wing and lead to disaster, one neglected pattern of drag can sabotage an entire destiny.

Look for the drag in your life, and be ruthless in dealing with it.

If you want to see what happens when drag is ruthlessly removed, watch the peregrine falcon, the fastest creature on earth. Its power doesn't come from extraordinary muscle. It comes from eliminating every form of drag, streamlining its body and cooperating magnificently with its unique shape and design.

Before it makes the dive that is faster than many planes, it folds its wings tight into its body, tucks its feet, flattens its feathers, aligns its head with its body, and transforms itself for minimal drag and maximal acceleration. The falcon is a living illustration of Hebrews 12:1:

> "Let us strip off every weight that slows us down."

To enter the next level of speed and impact, you must embrace the core concept of making things sleeker and simpler. You can't fly like a falcon with a life designed for hang gliding. Make a point of decluttering your schedule and saying "no" to opportunities regardless of their potential if they're not your assignment. Breakthroughs follow simplification, not the other way around.

Let go of responsibilities that you have outgrown. Simplify your product offering. Refocus your message. Sharpen your daily routine. It can be hard to change from the familiar and comfortable, laying aside what you've always done, but it's much harder living the rest of your life driving in a school zone when you know you were meant for speed!

The Seagull – The Power of Micro-Adjustments

As a child, I spent my school year on Georgian Bay (Lake Huron) and my summers at Lake Simcoe near Barrie, Ontario. Seagulls were a normal feature of daily life. If anything, they were a bit pesky, so I didn't notice the brilliance and skill behind their flight.

If you pay attention and know what to look for, you will see their constant micro-adjustments: subtle shifts in the angle of their wings, small changes in feather spacing, and minor tilts of the body that make them look a bit twitchy. If the wind is strong enough, a gull can appear to hover motionless, but if you look closely, there is a continuous flow of tiny corrections.

It is those highly skilled micro-adjustments that allow them to hold steady even in gusting winds, land skillfully atop a flagpole, and manage their way through blustering wind with ease. They gain their mastery not from frantically flapping their wings, but from countless small adjustments, tweaking their position on a second-by-second basis.

In life and business, most people want one big, beautiful decision to make everything smooth out, but it rarely works out that way. Instead, God is inviting us into a more intimate, moment-to-moment engagement with Him, making small adjustments to our course as we live out our day: a quick but sincere apology, a courtesy to a stranger in traffic, a short prayer with a colleague before a meeting, a softening of tone with your spouse, a daily practice of gratitude that, over time, orients your heart toward God, maybe even small incremental improvements in your sales process.

I watched my son run five-day promotions on his website. Each day, he would monitor conversion rates and if he wasn't satisfied with the number, he would tweak a headline, maybe change a graphic image, or text color. He could always tell when the change had an impact, and he would routinely average around 10,000 sales during each promotion. Individually, these seem trivial, which is why they are so overlooked. I sometimes think God hides rewards in lowly places to put them within reach of anyone who walks with enough humility to try them. If you make a series of micro-adjustments in the way you interact with your spouse, the way you proceed through a selling process, the drag that goes away will surprise you. Big doors swing on small hinges.

When God Deals with Drag

God is very aware of drag. He designed the birds to have minimal drag and maximum lift. When He invites us to cast all our cares on Him because He cares for us[2], that's an invitation to release emotional drag. He addresses relational drag by warning us not to be unequally yoked[3] and reminds us that "bad company corrupts good morals.[4]" And as I said earlier, Hebrews 12:1 addresses spiritual drag, urging us to...

> "lay aside every weight and the sin that so easily ensnares us."

Our mind is a big battlefield, and it creates perhaps more drag than anything else, which is why Paul tells us to be transformed by the renewing of our minds[5]. The drag from our poor sense of identity is dealt with in 2 Corinthians 5:17 with the promise that if anyone is in Christ, they are a new creation. Isaiah tells us to forget the former things because God is doing a new thing[6].

Most people want God to just give them more lift, more money, more prestige, more things, but quite often God provides that by reducing our drag. Relationships come to an end. Opportunities unrelated to our destiny evaporate. Position and rank in a company shift. Our schedule, once packed, lightens up. Even a demanding high-volume customer goes away, leaving a gaping hole in your business and your time.

What God means for good sometimes feels like loss. From God's perspective, He is scraping all the barnacles off, cutting all the overgrown vines that keep you earthbound. He is streamlining you for success, but it feels like He is stripping you bare to the bone.

John 15 calls it pruning. If you're not productive, He prunes you. If you are productive, He prunes you to produce more. Either way...

You're pruned if you do and pruned if you don't.
Blessed be the name of the Lord!

Before He raises you up, He sets you down and cuts away drag. Before He sends a warm thermal to lift you, He straightens feathers that would catch the wind and pull you off course.

Business in the Sky: The Science of Frictionless Sales

Birds reduce drag in order to survive. In business, you reduce drag (friction) to increase lift (revenue). For example, Amazon reduced drag by making buying effortless with one-click checkout, saved payment info, and free shipping in many cases to remove price hesitation. They became a trillion-dollar albatross, soaring on the thermals of frictionless sales that were not only fast, but smooth, and smooth creates trust, and trust creates lift.

Uber didn't invent the idea of hiring a car and driver to get you someplace, it removed the friction around it. No phone calls to central dispatch, no wondering when your ride would arrive, no handling of cash or awkward haggling over price. Tap, confirm, know the driver before they arrive, watch the car approach, step out when you arrive. Simple. Smooth. Lift.

Netflix did something similar in the entertainment industry by removing late fees, ending late-night trips to the store, and the hassle of rummaging through thousands of titles, by learning your preferences and suggesting options. These companies got massive lift by mastering what birds know instinctively: Make flying easier. Make buying easier. Make saying "yes" easier. People assume success is elusive but worth the effort. Birds prove that success belongs to anyone who removes the obstacles from the path.

Building Your Personal Lift System

If you want to rise in your calling and fulfill the destiny God has for you, then make it your mission to develop lift in the following four key dimensions of life. When these four realms align, life becomes a lot more aerodynamic.

1. **Spiritual lift** comes from intimacy with God. This is not about religious duty or obligation. It's about developing your relationship with God through time in His Word, worship that goes beyond songs into the surrender of your heart, prayer that is more interested in listening than in speaking, and willing obedience to His prompting.

2. **Emotional lift** is a choice that emerges from choosing gratitude, joy, forgiveness, healing, courage, hope, and seeing the best in others instead of the worst. It grows in a heart that takes no offense, practices being thankful, and brings wounds into the healing light of God's Presence.

3. **Mental lift** comes from clarity. Clarity allows for focus. Focus gives certainty. Certainty encourages action. Action produces results. Results are how we are measured. Measurement shows us where to improve. When you know what you are called to do, whom you are called to serve, and why it matters, your thoughts become streamlined, decisions become easier, and distractions lose their grip. A renewed mind makes transformation possible.

4. **Behavioral lift** flows out of mental clarity and institutes habits, routines, and disciplines that support your calling. It's about consistent

action in the right direction, doing the fundamentals in both your business and personal life.

The Goose V-Formation – Shared Lift, Shared Calling

One more flight pattern to complete the picture... Take a gander (pun intended) at a flock of geese traveling in the classic V-formation. Each goose, except the one in front, flies in the upwash created by the wingbeats of the bird ahead. This simple strategy reduces drag dramatically, by up to seventy percent, according to some studies. Because of that one strategy, the flock can travel farther and faster than any goose can fly on its own.

Naturally, the lead position is the most exhausting, so geese rotate. When the front bird gets worn out, it falls back and lets another take the lead position. This is a beautiful picture of what the Body of Christ and healthy business culture should look like. Mentors, partners, and teams create updraft. Being part of a mastermind, a church, a small group, or a committed leadership circle is equivalent to finding a V-formation in the sky. You don't lose your identity in the group; you gain efficiency and speed.

Isolation increases drag.
Community done right multiplies lift.

In business, like-hearted strategic alliances, the right joint ventures, and supportive networks keep you from burning out alone against the headwinds. Every visionary goes further when, on occasion, they have someone in front of them breaking the wind and carrying the load.

The Moment You Feel the Wind

Imagine you're standing at the North Rim of the Grand Canyon at dusk. Behind you lies the valley of your past: seasons of struggling in your own strength, projects weighed down by chaos and clutter, toxic relationships heavy with drag, years when gravity felt stronger than the grace God has extended. Ahead, beyond the far rim, is the future God has whispered in your spirit on those quiet nights beneath the stars. Above you, the warm air dissipates into the night sky. The remaining invisible thermals from the sunbaked, plowed fields are still faintly rising, and the gentle wind, almost untraceable, is still shifting and waiting.

Standing on the edge of this imaginary canyon rim, you extend your arms as if they were wings. You're about to leap, but before you do, you remember the albatross and refuse to resist what God sent to carry you. Then, like the hawk, you ask, "Lord... Where is the thermal? Where is the Spirit moving? Where is the Presence of God that I can ride upon and rise?"

You think for a moment about the falcon and choose to release the weights you've been dragging: the extra commitments, the fruitless projects, the hurts, and resentments. You envision the seagull and make a series of small decisions, to forgive, to let go and let God, to simplify life, to focus on what's important, to respond quickly, and to schedule time with God instead of just talking about it.

You sense, in the midst of all these choices, the quiet working of the Holy Spirit, the sure and certain voice of God, the wind of His Spirit pressing gently against the wings of your life. You know you can't control Him, but you do know that you can face in the right direction.

Then comes the moment of decision. You lean forward, tilting over the abyss. For a moment, nothing happens. Where is the wind?! Your stomach tightens. Your nerves start pinging. Your old familiar voice whispers forcefully, "Flap harder." Old fears demand your attention. They shout, "You're going to fall." But this time, instead of panicking, you keep your cool, you trust the proven process, and you hold your position of trust.

Then it comes. The wind catches. Lift overwhelms drag. You feel the unmistakable thrill of being carried. It's almost euphoric, but also calming. The ground begins to fall away as your elevation rises. You're moving, not because you're flapping frantically, but because you are positioned to catch the grace the wind affords. The forces that once intimidated you and held you back are now under your wings, working for you, just like God always intended!

You're really flying. Not because you flapped harder or tried longer, but because you learned how to trust. This is the law of birds: they succeed by obeying fixed laws of design, timing, trust, and rhythm. This is how God's Spirit works. It's how the kingdom of God works.

Birds demonstrate the beauty of flowing with the winds instead of struggling against them. They model how to rise by laws that favor us, so we don't have to fight against forces that resist us. But even the most effortless flight on a rising thermal requires something more...

Eyes that see. Instincts that discern. Awareness that reads the invisible. Birds can't soar safely if they don't perceive the shifting winds, the hidden predators, or the subtle changes in the environment around it.

Turn to Chapter Ten to learn how to see what others miss.

References: 1) 1 Corinthians 2:16 2) 1 Peter 5:7 3) 2 Corinthians 6:14 4) 1 Corinthians 15:33 5) Romans 12:2 6) Isaiah 43:19

CHAPTER 10

SEEING WHAT OTHERS MISS

Vigilance And Awareness

"The advantage so often goes to the one who sees what others miss."

I'm up most mornings before the sun touches the leaves of the highest oaks, and I get to see and hear what happens as the world shifts from night to day, from darkness to light.

Some days, I get to see the rising mist blanketing the small lake across the street, curling around the purple pickerelweed and sturdy cattails. Frogs have grown suspiciously silent. (They know something's up!) Insects are stirring. The entire natural world swings into motion.

Meantime, long before my wife rubs the sleep from her eyes or is greeted by our Labradoodle (finally allowed in to tell her how much he loves her) the birds are already very much awake and intensely aware. I'm not talking about merely being conscious of the new day and looking around. Birds are awake in a much more engaged way, fully tuned into the environment with a level of attentiveness that rivals our highest moments of focus – only for them, it is the default setting.

At this early hour, I am not too perky. I sleepily make my way to the bathroom, splash cold water on my face, run a brush through my hair, and head to the kitchen to make some pre-dawn coffee, which I slowly consume as I feed my soul.

Birds, however, begin their day in a posture of vigilance. Their eyes scan the landscape, their ears sort through the multiple layers of sound, and their whole body becomes a living intelligence-gathering center.

Vigilance. Awareness. An acute sensitivity to imperceptible cues. An intuitive assessment of the morning's environment. This is a level of perception mastery that keeps them alive in danger and points them to potential treasure troves of provision for the day. The very capacity they have to succeed in their environment is the same capacity that separates leaders from followers, because in business and life...

The advantage so often goes to the one
who sees what others miss.

This chapter is about that advantage.

Allow me to introduce you to the tiny warden of the forest, the Carolina Wren. Weighing only about three-quarters of an ounce, this adorable, cinnamon-colored creature lives in forests filled with predators. They have to watch out for hawks circling overhead, owls discreetly scanning the forest with their incredible eyesight, foxes or raccoons looking for a snack, even a snake slithering beneath the leaf-covered forest floor.

It's just another day for this little one, and it's not afraid. The wren is no match for the predators. It has small claws instead of powerful talons, a small beak that looks meek, no protective armor, and certainly not enough size to chase predators away. What it does have is awareness, something we would do well to cultivate in our own lives.

A wren can hear the faintest rustle of a snake making its way through dead leaves before the snake is close enough to strike. Unbelievably, the wren can detect the minuscule pressure change when a hawk is gliding through the canopy. When an insect twitches beneath the bark of a tree, the wren notices.

Watch the wren closely and you'll notice its tail flicking and body moving in a way that looks like nervous energy, but is not. It is maintaining a posture of readiness, ready to fly away to safety, or breakfast, at the slightest hint of a threat or opportunity.

Most of the wren's vigilance reveals neither threat nor provision, but when either surface, it's totally prepared to act. Their strategy is simple... See early, respond early. Notice danger before it attacks. Perceive opportunities hidden beneath a layer of forest debris. Act while others are still wondering what happened.

The wren is modeling a sermon without speech, that there's more to success than hard work. You can't succeed if you become someone else's prey. Success is also a matter of acute watchfulness.

Your life will be molded by what you notice
and quietly destroyed by what you don't.

Why do good, competent leaders fail? It's not usually because they lacked vision or didn't work hard at their calling. More often than not, it's because they didn't see the early warning signs, whether that was their own cold heart, their team dynamics, or the financial warnings.

I've seen it more often than I'd like to admit, but when companies fail, it's not because they weren't working hard. It's not because there were no signals. It's because no one was paying attention to them. The signs were there, but ignored. The prize doesn't always go to the strongest, fastest, or smartest. It's the reward for the watchful, those who are paying attention, analyzing threats, and looking for opportunities.

Scripture backs this up in multiple places, none more vividly than when Peter says,

> "Be sober, be vigilant; because your adversary the devil walks about like a roaring lion, seeking whom he may devour.[1]"

Hosea laments that God's people perish, not because they don't work hard, but because of lack of knowledge[2]. Knowledge comes through observation. It happens at the INPUT stage previously mentioned.

Throughout the Hebrew text, the word "shamar" runs like a silver thread of promise. It means to keep, to guard, to observe, to attend. It describes the duty of priests who were to guard the temple, the role of shepherds to watch their flocks by night, and the habit of prophets like Habakkuk standing on the city walls[3], probing the horizon with their watchful eyes looking for signs of danger or deliverance. This is not casual observation on a stroll... It's intentional, focused awareness.

God gifted birds their own version of "shamar". It's built into their nervous system, but you and I have to choose it, develop it, and live by it, because in life and in business,

You rise to the level of your awareness
and fall to the level of your neglect.

We tend to prosper in relation to what we perceive. A bird that fails to "shamar" becomes breakfast for a more alert predator. A person who is not vigilant becomes a victim of avoidable mistakes and easy prey for a competitor in the marketplace.

Opportunity doesn't park outside your home with a big neon sign. It is subtle. It whispers. When it comes your way discreetly, that's because it's meant only for you. It shows up in patterns that others miss, curious circumstances that others brush off. Destruction behaves in a similar way, and by the time most people see it approaching, it's too late to avoid the worst of the damage.

Vigilance is how you go from being caught off guard and experiencing the consequences of that, to cooperating with God and participating in the banquet He has prepared for you in the presence of your enemies.

The Robin and the Hidden Opportunity

The robin is impressive for its ability to see the unseeable. Instead of seeing from afar, it specializes in seeing what lies beneath. That is no small feat. I've seen robins hopping around the yard, pausing, tilting their head, listening, and then suddenly driving their beak beneath the surface of the ground and pulling out a worm. When you see it in action, it looks like a magician pulling a rabbit out of a hat. But it's not magic.

They are expert opportunity seekers and look where others do not bother. They reach into the realm of the unseen and pull out provision as if they were at the grocery store reaching for something on the shelf. The secret is out however. They don't have advance knowledge of the worm's location. They're able to detect minuscule vibrations in the soil that disclose the worm's clandestine location.

Their entire body becomes a listening instrument, attuned to signals most creatures overlook, from the way they tilt their head to detect sound at the perfect angle, to the keenness of their vision and patient observation. Worms aren't known for their speed. They crawl, but as long as they're moving, they are detectable.

The wren's vigilance is primarily fear-based due to its vulnerability to predators, but the robin's vigilance is much more opportunity-based. Like a scene from The Hunt for Red October with Sean Connery, where the men in submarines are using every tool they have to listen for the other side to make a noise, robins watch for the faintest of signs to indicate that provision is at hand, even though it may not yet be visible.

This is how many breakthroughs are discovered. They often begin with what feels like a hunch, but that hunch has its genesis in something subtle they picked up on. A change in the way customers talk, recurring problems that are usually overlooked, a change in buying patterns or product preferences. Maybe something trending on social media. Instead of passing over these clues, learn from the robin and pause, pay attention, scratch beneath the surface, and see if what you're sensing has anything to it. People who investigate those subtle signals tend to be the ones who launch the next innovation, be that a product or service, or get the promotion on the job for the next strategic role.

Proverbs says,

> "The hearing ear and the seeing eye, the Lord has made them both.[4]"

We tend to think of those only in the physical sense, but seeing and hearing are also spiritual gifts that can give us strategic advantage in the marketplace. When most competitors have limited themselves to the naturally observable world, you can have the advantage of a second set of eyes that Paul calls "the eyes of your understanding[5]" and the gift of hearing what others with ears do not hear[6]. The gift of strategic seeing and hearing must be used if you're going to get any value from them.

Opportunity favors the perceptive.

So it makes sense to use every perceptive ability God has provided. Success in life and the prosperity that goes with it often flows to those willing to pay attention to what others overlook.

The breakthrough you seek may well be just below the surface of your current assignment. The question is whether you're listening or just hearing, and whether you're discerning or just seeing!

The Nightingale and the Art of Hearing Guidance

In Hosea 4:6, God said, "My people are destroyed because of lack of knowledge", which brings me to the nightingale, an extraordinary bird that has a repertoire of over a thousand distinct song variations, making it one of the most accomplished vocalists in the bird world, capable of hearing and reproducing intricate patterns of pitch, rhythm, and harmony that the average person could never decipher.

So, maybe you're wondering what the connection is to success and how it relates to vigilance. Well, here it is... Vigilance is not limited to visual cues, it's also about hearing guidance beyond the audible level.

A lot of failures are not because someone didn't see the danger, but rather because of what they refused to hear. Let that sink in.

In 1982, I had the opportunity to jump into a well-funded, promising business partnership. The stars seemed aligned, but on the inside, I had a strong sense that if I proceeded, it would be like jumping into a giant blender and turning it on. I proceeded anyway and was completely shredded. I refused to hear the warning bells going off on the inside.

Don't make that mistake. You've had that inner guidance too. "This deal is not right." "Don't marry him." "Take this job." "Put your home on the market." etc., and you argued with your intuition and lost.

Maybe it's just a recurring nudge toward taking a certain action, but you don't understand why, so you delay until it's too late. Some people say that God is the God of second chances, but I'm here to tell you:

There are no second chances.
Just different chances.

The nightingale demonstrates that awareness is a multi-sensory experience. Here's how... Most creatures rely on vision during the day, and that capacity weakens substantially at night. The nightingale, however, thrives in the night, singing most powerfully in the dark, when vision is greatly limited, forcing them to rely on other senses.

When their vision ability is reduced, they rely on...

- hearing to detect rivals, mates, and potential threats,
- spatial memory – those mental maps of the territory they have staked out,
- vibration and resonance – how sound moves through the air and bounces off the foliage,
- timing and pattern recognition (responding to the calls of others), and
- their own internal state of being (awareness, energy, and readiness).

When you develop your spiritual, emotional, and intuitive hearing, it may require you to make decisions that others will not understand. That's okay. They'll catch up with you later. You may choose to pass on a deal that looks good when the presenter is spinning circles on a white board, but on the inside, you know that it's not a fit for you.

The person who has learned to listen to the full spectrum of INPUT God has made available to them is not afraid to make an unexpected U-turn or pivot into a direction of uncharted territory. They've come to depend on the promise Jesus made, that...

> "My sheep hear My voice, and I know them, and they follow Me."[7]

But, in order to hear, in order to tune into the Spirit, you need to quiet the external noise and the inner battle that often rages. The world is constantly offering up fear, urgency, conflict, jealousy, and meaningless distractions. Vigilance means purposefully tuning your ear to hear what the Spirit is saying.

For me, the best way to turn down the competing noise is to marinate my mind in the Scriptures. That's when I hear Him best.

The Kingfisher and Adaptive Vision

You might remember the kingfisher from a previous chapter. Not only is it sleek, wearing its feathers like a brightly colored, form-fitting superhero outfit, but it is an amazingly effective hunter. He hunts fish from a perch above the water, waiting for the right fish to come near the surface. Then he dives headfirst into the water, making his body the shaft of a powerful spear and his beak, the tip of the spear, hitting the water at 60 miles per hour.

The sleekness of his dive is made possible by the design God gave it, but it doesn't use its beak to impale the fish as many have thought. That spear-like design is for efficiency under water. Once underwater, it uses its beak like a powerful pair of tweezers.

Kingfishers weigh only ounces, depending on the species, so they use their design to succeed by accuracy over brute force, timing over raw strength, and design matched to the environment they live in.

They don't get into a wrestling match with the fish, they intercept it at precisely the right moment. This is a bird that demonstrates mastery of the design God gave it, instead of trying to catch fish like an eagle does.

But I haven't even got to the good part yet! Have you ever noticed when you try to reach for something in water, and it's not exactly where your eyes perceived it to be? That's because light bends when it passes from air into water. If the kingfisher didn't somehow adjust his vision going from air to water, it would miss its prey every time.

So, God equipped the kingfisher with a transparent eyelid that closes mid-dive, protecting its eye when it hits water, acting like a high-tech diving mask. It also shifts the shape of its eye and adjusts the position of its lenses to correct for refraction, enabling it to see differently than it does above water. Pretty impressive!

The big takeaway from its adaptation of vision from one environment to another is the lesson that you need to adjust how you look at things depending on the conditions at hand. Is the business in need of triage, or is it well established looking for new acquisitions? Is this a startup with limited cash and no proof of concept, or a well-financed venture with proven market demand?

The filter you view circumstances through needs to adapt to the circumstances you're in. Before pulling out your trusty solution from a previous victory, ask yourself, "What environment am I in right now?" The lens you view life through needs to adapt to current realities. Using the same cookie-cutter strategy over and over again will not work in shifting environments. Are you in a temporary trial, or is this a change of seasons for you? Ask God to reveal that to you. The kingfisher doesn't insist that everything look the same underwater as it does above. It adjusts to the environment. So should you.

The Owl's Uncanny Discernment

After the sun has slipped below the horizon and the long shadows of the forest become a nighttime blanket of darkness, most birds fall silent. Filling the silence of the songbirds is the newly awakened sound of crickets and frogs, coyotes and foxes, that come to life and keep the forest alive with sound.

Have you ever seen an owl perched on a limb? They look like lawmen keeping a watch on every movement and motive in the forest, and are uniquely equipped for their role. Their asymmetrical ears are positioned at slightly different heights so they can triangulate sound in three dimensions, giving them hearing so exact, they can locate a mouse scurrying beneath a layer of leaves or even snow. But there's more.

Have you ever seen their face? It looks like they got smashed by an iron skillet, giving them a somewhat rounded face that actually funnels sound toward their ears like a satellite dish. Their enormous eyes are forward-facing, gathering every available photon of light. I'm not making fun of these guys, they are a bit creepy looking, but who am I to judge one of God's amazing creatures? (-: The thing is though; they can hunt successfully in conditions where other competitors hear and see nothing. For the owl, the night is not shutdown mode, it is full of information that they can take complete advantage of. They were made for the night!

Their ability to hear what others can't, and see what others miss is what spiritual discernment looks like. When Paul prays that believers would "abound in knowledge and depth of insight, so that you may approve what is excellent,[8]" he is asking God to give them the ability to discern and detect truth in conditions where others are confused, to perceive the subtle signs of deception and threat, and to recognize the quiet footsteps of hidden opportunity.

In your life there are times when seeing the path forward is difficult. Markets shift, trends change, algorithms flip, crisis comes out of nowhere, or maybe God is leading you into unfamiliar territory that has no familiar markers or relationships to lean on. In times like that, worldly wisdom and natural observation are insufficient.

You need discernment and keen hearing to hear what the Spirit is whispering to you so that you don't shut down or respond irrationally in panic, but instead rely on the spiritual insight God gives you. Spiritual awareness and the courage to act separates those who are paralyzed by uncertainty and fear of the unknown from those who can navigate through it.

The Dove and Awareness Without Anxiety

Doves are among the most gentle and peaceful birds on the planet, but they maintain a constant state of awareness in their environment. They can share a city park or city square with other birds, dogs, and people, even cars and trucks. They're not oblivious to the world around them, but they're not paranoid either. They carefully observe the environment and they read intent. They want to know whether they're being stalked, or if this person approaching, is friendly?

Doves have no guile. They don't ambush, use trickery to steal food, or deceive rivals with fake signals. Their behavior is straightforward, unfeigned, and predictable. When Jesus instructs us to be "harmless as doves", He's not talking about weakness, passivity, or willful naivety.

The dove is predictably gentle because
it is unpolluted by aggression.

Have you ever known someone that easily "flies off the handle" or goes from a smile to rage quicker than you can say "Bob's your uncle"? Maybe it happens in traffic, but you never know when something might set them off.

Doves are not reactive in that way. They don't escalate tension or respond to threats with threats. Their nervous system is not wired for rage cycles. They don't live in fear, they simply refuse to be hijacked by it. It's not in their nature to retaliate because there is no violence within that can be awakened.

When Jesus says to be wise as serpents (aware, discerning with foresight) and harmless as doves, the admonition is to be fully aware of your surroundings, without becoming tainted by what you see or hear. This goes back to the INPUT stage mentioned earlier in the book. Guard what you watch or listen to, because it affects what develops on the inside and ultimately who and what you become on the outside.

Vigilance with a polluted heart becomes anxiety.

Peace without vigilance begets gullibility leading to destruction. The dove carries both peace and vigilance, a powerful combination, leading to success and the avoidance of defeating pitfalls that so many experience. In business, vigilance looks like paying attention to trends, tracking key performance indicators, monitoring customer experience, etc. Success often comes to the person who notices early, interprets rightly, and can adapt quickly. When you become the most aware person in the room, who knows the data, understands current market sentiment, sees how God is working, and knows what to do with that input, you become invaluable[9].

Once you set your mind and disposition to be vigilant, your senses sharpen, and you can spot a fake a mile away. You see hidden agendas that are masked over with flattery. You recognize the distractions coming your way that are much more subtle and strategic than you used to think. You can read the spiritual atmosphere in the room and recognize manipulation as it forms in conversation. Allow your vigilance to be honed, guided, and informed by the Holy Spirit.

The Weaponization of Distraction

I have a theory about this. After the resurrection of Jesus, John said,

> "We know that we are of God, and the whole world lies under the sway of the wicked one.[10]"

Paul clarified further when he said that our battle is not with mere men, but rather with unseen forces in heavenly places[11].

When you're discerning a situation and detect a hidden agenda that looks like kindness, but is really a masked attempt to use you for personal gain, be aware that the enemy of your soul is not going after your stuff. He is using the weakness of the other party and their lust for gain, to motivate them to accomplish his purpose, which is to keep you distracted from the good works which God prepared beforehand that you should walk in[12].

If he can get you into things like anger, resentment, retaliation, self-pity, bitterness, or fear, you will miss what God has for you in that moment. If you stay in that mode, you will miss out on your higher purpose, and the mission that was meant for you will pass to another.

That brings me to what I call the weaponization of distraction. We now live in a world dominated by distraction. Modern life has been engineered to keep you distracted. Our phones ding and chirp with alerts. Apps compete for your dopamine, the control of your motivation system. Screens flash. News cycles spin. Busyness masquerades as productivity. We're inundated with so much noise that we've forgotten (if we ever knew) how to respond to God's invitation to...

> "Behold the works of the Lord... Be still and know that I am God.[13]"

As God said to Cain in Genesis 4,

> "Sin lies at the door. And its desire is for you, but you should rule over it.[14]"

We must consciously choose the INPUT that we allow to have the attention of our eyes, ears, and thoughts. We must renew the desire, and recover the ability to sit quietly, think deeply, and to observe without immediately responding. Remember when Jesus learned that His friend Lazarus was near death? He didn't rush to the scene. He stayed where He was for two more days. In a world full of urgent needs and mosquito-like distractions, the ability to maintain focus and stay on mission is a superpower.

Social media invites you to "like" and "follow" many things, most of which don't matter. Birds don't make that mistake. They don't track everything, only what matters, and then act accordingly. We don't need to know everything about everything. We need to stay highly aware of the few things that relate to the priorities God has given us, our own spiritual condition, the tone we set for our home and business, the direction of our calling, and those we are responsible for.

In truth, awareness is a cultivated spiritual gift that may mean survival in one circumstance, opportunity in another, or just an invitation from God to join Him in something He's doing. Awareness at its best is alignment with the Lord who sees and knows the end from the beginning.

Be watchful. Be alert. See early.
Discern early. Interpret early. Act early.

Awareness gives you a tremendous advantage in life, protecting you from danger, guiding you through turbulence, and positioning you for opportunity. Decide today to be vigilant, watchful, and fully aware. It is key to your destiny!

Acceleration is exhilarating, but to maintain it, requires more than awareness, it requires strategic relationships properly aligned with your God-given direction. Momentum multiplies more in community than in solitude. Direction gains confirmation in unity. Speed increases when complementary strengths are aligned in singleness of purpose.

Turn the page to Chapter Eleven and learn about the power of multiplied momentum.

References: 1) 1 Peter 5:8. 2) Hosea 4:6 3) Habakkuk 2:1 4) Proverbs 20:12 5) Ephesians 1:18 6) Mark 4:9 7) John 10:27 8) Philippians 1:10 9) 1 Chronicles 12:32 10) 1 John 5:19. 11) Ephesians 6:12 12) Ephesians 2:10 13) Psalm 46:8 & 10 14) Genesis 4:7

CHAPTER 11

THE POWER OF MULTIPLIED MOMENTUM

Flock Synergy

"Isolation weakens and depletes, while unity strengthens and multiplies."

Nature is a demonstration of God's wisdom in practice. We have the opportunity to witness that wisdom and translate it into beneficial outcomes for our lives. While not every bird habit easily gives up the wisdom behind it, one of the easiest to observe, understand, and practice happens early in the autumn.

The air starts to develop an edge as the annual cool down begins, and the wind that earlier was a welcome breeze on a hot summer day has developed a bit of a bite. The light is fading faster these days as it makes its exit over freshly harvested fields. If you happen to be standing outside, you may hear it before you see it, a distant honking that invites your attention.

As the sky dims the light even further, a shape comes into view. At first, it's just a slight discoloration against the once blue sky, but as it draws closer, the shape comes into focus. It's not Winston Churchill with his famous "V" for victory sign, nor is it a giant "V" shaped alien spacecraft. As the honking sound gets louder, that smudge of an image sharpens into an unmistakable flying "V", cutting through the dusky heavens like a returning army after a victory.

It's not a stray goose or two flying aimlessly southward. It's a flock of geese piercing the air like a living arrowhead, with wings beating to a rhythm they alone can hear. Many hearts, one mission, moving in coordination that is instinctive to them and instructive to us. Each goose has its own body, past experiences, and expectations, yet together they become something far larger than the sum of their parts. They have one unified purpose, one predetermined direction, and one migration to complete. They are doing instinctively what people are hesitant to do.

They combine their strength without
neutralizing their individuality.

They share leadership responsibilities without a power struggle. They fly in sync with each other, an army of one, without losing their identity or giving up their personal goals to nest, mate, and raise little goslings. As a flock in formation, they're able to travel much further than if flying alone.

God gave them the gift of flight, but the genius of flying in formation is God's way of tipping His hand to reveal a secret. This chapter is about that secret... That birds fly higher, further, and faster in flocks, and so can you. Your calling in life, the business you have, the ministry you aspire to, your family, and your destiny itself were never meant to be lived out in solitude. Scripture says that

> "God sets the solitary in families; He brings out those who are bound into prosperity;[1]"

This chapter is your invitation to rediscover the synergistic power of the flock.

The Masterpiece in the Sky

It happens every year as summer fades, autumn cools, and winter turns the lights out. Untold millions of birds leave the familiarity of home and make an epic journey, some crossing countries, others crossing continents, and some migrations span entire oceans. It's not just geese or ducks. It's tiny sandpipers and arctic terns, warblers and storks, ruby-throated hummingbirds, owls, orioles, and more.

They leave the familiar and trace highways in the sky they alone can see, not with their eyes, but with their internal navigation system. The route they take and the destination they're headed for are encoded in a memory they have yet to live. Each species follows their own unique pattern that works best for the design they came into the world with.

Geese famously emblazon the sky with "V's" while pelicans travel in single file, forming a straight line across the sky as if drawn by a ruler. Sandhill cranes arrive in Florida stretched in a formation that mirrors the slight curve of the earth. European starlings swirl and spin in thick, shape shifting formations called murmurations, turning the sky into a virtual movie screen, while the tiny bar-tailed godwits fly nonstop from Alaska to New Zealand often in cohesive, unified groups.

Not one of these birds decides to pack up and migrate on their own. They travel together as one, they survive together as one, and succeed together as one because they know instinctively that...

Isolation weakens and depletes,
while unity strengthens and multiplies.

Companies, churches, nations, even families rise or fall on this law. A highly talented individual can make some noise, but a unified flock can literally change the landscape when thousands upon thousands of birds stop by a field for lunch, or perhaps while relieving themselves in flight, drop seeds that later become trees where there were none. Over time, they open new territories, establish permanent routes, and create predictable flyways that preserve momentum.

Of all the various migratory formations, none is more iconic than the "V" formation geese are famous for doing. Except for the goose in front, each bird in that formation flies slightly above and behind the bird ahead, allowing it to fly in the upwash that follows the leader's wingbeats.

Each bird benefits from the effort of the one in front of it, reducing their energy expenditure by up to 70%. With those energy savings, they can fly two or three times further on the same energy reserve. By flying in shared alignment, they cover more distance at greater speeds than any maverick bird traveling alone could ever hope for.

Solomon spoke of the power of unity in this way:

> "Two are better than one, because they have a good reward for their labor, for if they fall, one will lift up his companion. But woe to him who is alone when he falls, for he has no one to help him up... Though one may be overpowered by another, two can withstand him. And a threefold cord is not quickly broken.[2]"

For those who could not read, they could always pay attention to the sermon in the sky, observing how proper alignment produces lift, and unity generates multiplication.

Practically speaking, any company where individuals or departments isolate or pull in different directions, will slow momentum, and blur the corporate vision. Any ministry where leaders operate with competing visions will lose impact and followers. In a marriage where husband and wife do their own thing and never fly in formation, they often end up in different destinations, wondering how they "grew apart". But anytime people in a group, rally around a shared vision and are willing to serve in ways that lift others, they will travel further and faster than individual talent will ever take them.

As any leader knows, there is a cost to being the tip of the spear. The lead goose faces the full force of the wind as it breaks the air for those behind it. As glamorous as leadership may appear to some, it burns more energy than any other position on the team. The leader is the most exposed, most criticized, and hardest hit when things don't go smoothly. In geese migration, this energy drain is alleviated by rotating leadership. When the lead goose tires, it simply drifts back along one side of the "V", allowing another goose to step up into the lead position. In this way, leadership is rotational, burdens are shared, and status takes a back seat to mission.

I saw this play out in 1985 when I attended a new church planting in Langley, British Columbia. After attending a couple of services, I still didn't know who the pastor was. There were only a few dozen attendees at most, but no apparent leader. I was just a visitor, but upon inquiry I learned that the point position was shared by a team. Each week, a different member of the small leadership team would be responsible for the flow of the service and the preaching of the Word.

Shortly after visiting this unusual church, I headed to America where I married and took up residence. However, I checked back with a friend a couple months later to see if that church was still going. It had grown nearly tenfold in about three months. That rapid growth continued, with multiple related but autonomous churches springing up in the area, truly transforming the landscape of the region. That movement, originally birthed out of California, developed into thousands of likeminded congregations globally.

Contrast that to what we've seen too often, where one ego driven person clings to the front until they collapse from exhaustion or fall into disrepute. Strong leaders need strong leaders. Moses needed Hur to lift his arms. David needed mighty men in positions of leadership. Paul traveled with Barnabas, Silas, Timothy, and others for mutual strengthening and partnership in the spreading of the gospel.

Good leaders know when to step out front and when to rest, when to take the reins and when to let competent leaders own some responsibility. It can look like sharing the platform to develop emerging leaders in the organization, instead of going solo on every occasion. In family life, it can mean recognizing when one spouse has the emotional bandwidth to lead in a given circumstance or season of life, and letting that happen. Longevity is fostered in the context of community, not celebrity.

One of the least known but powerful lessons from flock synergy is when a goose falls out of formation due to injury or sickness.

As the injured or sick goose drifts to the ground, two healthy geese will also drop out of formation and follow it to the ground, where they will guard it, warm it, and protect it as much as they can.

They will stay with their companion until it is ready to rejoin the migration in another formation, or until it dies. Then and only then will they rejoin the migration. They are modeling truth in action. Solomon said it this way...

> "A friend loves at all times, and a brother is born for adversity,[3]"

Jesus said in John 15:13,

> "Greater love has no one than this, than to lay down one's life for his friends."

These birds with no record of church attendance or seminary training, model the gospel more faithfully than many who do.

The Mesmerizing Wisdom of Starlings

Geese demonstrate unity in the structure they adhere to, but starlings demonstrate unity in their highly synchronized movements, called murmurations. They swirl by the thousands in a breathtaking spectacle of choreographed movement that makes Cirque Du Soleil look like amateur hour. I've seen thousands of them unify to appear like a giant bird hundreds of yards in size, before shape shifting into a silhouette of something unrecognizable, but arranged purposefully.

Their secret for unity in movement across thousands of birds is to simply pay attention to the six or seven starlings closest to it. When they respond to small changes in the inner circle closest to them, it contributes to the unity and flow of the flock. Unlike geese, there is no leader at the front dictating direction. Leadership is distributed, awareness is universal, made possible by synchronized attentiveness.

In a company, if everyone understands the mission and the vision, and regularly reflects on that, their individual movements will be in alignment despite not being in contact with every other member of the team. They need only be responsible for their actions consistent with the larger vision, and make sure their close teammates are following suit.

The starling principle does not require micromanagement. It requires tightly knit groups actively paying attention to one another, responding quickly, and aligning their daily tasks with the larger mission, vision, and shared values. A business where everyone depends on the CEO for direction while they labor away in silos will bottleneck quickly, while a business where each team stays in communication with the others closest to them and adjusts quickly as needed will thrive, even in times of turbulence.

At age fifteen I had a summer job working on a 4,000-acre farm in Carnduff, Saskatchewan. My job was to cultivate the fields, plowing up the fallow ground. I remember the birds that would come to feed and forage for insects. One such bird, the Western Meadowlark, is considered the "prairie icon" because it is such a common summer resident. If you watch carefully, you will see a small flock descend to the field and begin their foraging while one bird perches on a nearby fencepost. He refrains from eating because he is on duty, scanning the sky and the horizon for threats like foxes or hawks. Upon seeing danger, it gives a sharp call, and the entire group explodes into flight to take cover or reposition.

One bird's vigilance became everyone's protection. They understand that they survive not just on their own wits, but through shared awareness. People who always insist on doing things on their own, all too often find out too late that the "freedom" they sought is really a set up for disaster. It may look heroic at first glance, but prolonged DIY living has a cost, and sometimes that cost is everything.

Swallows are a fascinating bird capable of astonishing aerial acrobatics as they chase insects in flight, maneuvering with stunning agility. As impressive as their speed is, they move even faster when drafting off each other's wake, anticipating each other's twists and turns, and riding the shared currents they create.

Their unity becomes velocity.

Unity is not just a warm fuzzy feeling. It is a practical accelerator. When any group synchronized to the same vision and mission coordinates their collective efforts, they complete projects quicker and momentum builds.

Consider the power of what we see in Acts 2 where believers were all together in one place and in one accord. The Holy Spirit fell on a room full of people whose hearts were in tune together, so much so, that after that, they devoted themselves to teaching, to fellowship, to prayer, and to breaking bread, resulting in an acceleration of the spreading of the gospel that turned the world upside down[4].

In Scripture, Jesus identifies Himself as the good shepherd and we are the flock of sheep He watches over. The lost are portrayed as wandering sheep[5]. When a sheep wanders off, the shepherd with a hundred sheep, will leave the ninety-nine, to find the one that was lost, because we were meant to thrive in community, not in separation.

Paul compares the church to a body with many parts, each with different functions, but one Spirit, making the point that no one reaches maturity in isolation[6]. Growth is a team activity and calling is fulfilled in community.

NASA's Apollo program put men on the moon not because of one genius in Houston, but because tens of thousands of engineers, technicians, administrators, and astronauts aligned their efforts in a single direction. Elite military units like Navy SEAL teams succeed not because they recruit superheroes, but because they train intensely for trust, communication, and mutual protection. Their mantra, "no one left behind," is what we see modeled by geese in migration.

In the wild, predators rarely charge the center of the herd, choosing instead the isolated, the wounded, the slow movers. Isolation is deceptive. At first it feels like freedom, but it is actually exposure and elevated risk. God designed human success to function the same way bird success does: strength in numbers, vulnerability in isolation.

When a bird in isolation flaps its wings, only its body moves. When a flock forms, synergy is unleashed and energy compounds. Jesus talked about the power of even a small flock where two or three are gathered in His name, because He promised to be in their midst. Any team aligned around a God inspired vision can accomplish in a year what a host of scattered individuals can accomplish in a decade.

As the sun sinks below the distant horizon, turning the dazzling blue sky to yellow, then orange, and finally a deep purple, something in the world of geese resting in a marsh begins to stir. A goose lifts its head as if to ask, "Does anyone else sense what I'm sensing?" Another responds by lifting its wings, inspiring others to do the same. Soon the entire flock has lifted up from the marsh, headed to parts unknown.

They will fly together, feed together, cross borders and continents together, face the same storms together, and course correct together when knocked off their route by severe winds. They will take turns at leadership, trade places often, honk out loud encouragement along the way, and if necessary, leave the sky to sit beside a sick or wounded companion. They will do what they were made to do, face life together, riding the same wind over the same water, year after year, as a living example for others to emulate.

We were made for something very similar. We were meant for community, to live life in relationship with others. We were never intended to be the ego centric, superhero, lone ranger type that lives alone, works alone, and dies alone. You were never meant to fly alone. You were designed for covenant, for community, and to harness the synergy of the flock to multiply the momentum God has for you.

God sets the solitary in families[7] to multiply impact and strengthen the individual. Families or teams that flock together, stay together, and fulfill the purpose of God for their lives. Unity gives you power for the journey, but fearless trust powers your soul.

In Chapter Twelve, step into the mystery of confidence in the unseen God who carries us farther than our own strength or teamwork ever could.

References: 1) Psalm 68:6 2) Ecclesiastes 4:9-12 3) Proverbs 17:17 4) Acts 17:6. 5) Luke 15:4. 6) 1 Corinthians 12 7) Psalm 68:6

CHAPTER 12

THE FLIGHT OF CONFIDENCE

Fearless Trust

"If you can believe, all things are possible to him that believes." (Mark 9:23)

We see it so frequently that we seldom give it serious consideration. It happens on rooftops and branches, fence posts and power lines. A small bird adjusts its position, scans the horizon, pauses for just a moment, and then it does something man has always wanted to do...

It leaps.

It doesn't leap with timidity or a sense of fear. It's not overcoming a bad case of "what ifs". There's no attempt to somehow cut a deal with gravity to give it a break, nor is it doing mathematical calculations on wind speed and direction, air density, humidity levels, and distance to the ground. It simply leaps off as naturally as it drew its previous breath.

It doesn't test the air with a wing tip, nor does it second guess the design of the wings it has. It doesn't ask for or receive any written guarantee. It simply does what it was designed to do, and the best part is, it feels so natural. It entrusts its wellbeing to an invisible support it cannot see, nor measure, and certainly cannot control.

The bird most likely marvels at people who walk instead of fly. Perhaps they joke about it while chirping on the nearby tree limb. For them, this is simply life. Every single day they model faith by leaping off a secure branch, totally worry free, into an environment they can't see, but know somehow that it will support them.

Birds by nature operate on a level of faith that people often lack. It's a fearless confidence that the air they cannot see will hold them, that provision they have not yet found will show up when needed, that they are equipped to navigate through danger, and that flight is as certain as the rising sun. They live inside the promise of the Sermon on the Mount that most people, at best, can only quote.

In Matthew 6:26, Jesus said, "Behold the birds of the air… your heavenly Father feeds them". He didn't say to glance at them. He said "Behold". Study. Observe. Learn. Because birds are much more than background decoration to enhance our view. They are living metaphors of profound truth, winged instructors demonstrating what it looks like to live worry-free when trust replaces fear. Fear is drag, but trust is lift. Birds choose trust every time, and every single time, they get lift.

Imagine for a moment what your life would look like
if you had that same level of confidence.

What if you believed that whatever you put your hand to would prosper[1]? How would that change things for you? What great things would you aspire to accomplish?

This chapter explores the power of fearless trust, what Scripture offers those who possess it, and what you can accomplish with it. Spoiler alert: Jesus Himself said,

> "If you can believe, all things are possible to him that believes.[2]"

Yep, we're going there too. Sadly, we've turned that verse into a motivational slogan, but rarely inhabit it or operate from it.

That changes here and now. Read on...

All Things Are Possible... (Not Necessarily Probable)

I admit that I have quoted Mark 9:23 many times and said I believed it, but was unable to consistently produce what I said I "believed". That can be a hard pill to swallow. Can you relate? It is 100% fixable when you understand that biblical belief is not intellectual agreement, it is alignment, where what you say aligns with your deep inner beliefs and corresponding outer actions.

Corresponding Action

I was in my twenties and flat broke after my daughter died. Not long after that, I lost my first real business, my marriage, my homes, and car, etc., and was staying at a friend's home for survival. I was desperate to see God rescue me.

One evening, I went to a home meeting where another young man was asking for prayer for his knee. After folks prayed for him, they broke for coffee and cookies. I was pretty cynical at that time and thought to myself, if he really had faith to be healed, he would jump up NOW and do what he couldn't previously do.

At that moment, the Holy Spirit challenged me to do the same kind of thing regarding my finances. I was two months behind on a bank loan payment and they wanted paid and kept calling me. I felt like the Holy Spirit challenged me to do what I was critical of the young man for not doing. I was to take the action corresponding to my "belief" that God would help me financially, but I had no job, no money, and no source of income.

So, I determined that first thing the next morning, I would drive to the bank, ask for the loan officer handling my account, tell him I had the money for payments (roughly $1,500), and then open my wallet and start counting out the cash. What made this idea challenging was that I had less than $20 in my wallet. But I determined to do exactly that, knowing that I would appear to be either a fool or a deceiver if I told the loan officer I had the money in my wallet, opened it up to pay him, and there was nothing there.

The next morning, without telling anyone my predicament or intentions, I headed off to do just that. No one knew I was two months behind on my bank payment because it's just not the kind of thing you tell folks.

On my way to the bank, I stopped by the place where I had been staying to get something. While there, I ran into a good friend who said that he had just been seeking the Lord that morning and he said, God told him he was supposed to give me a check. It was for $2,000. I carried on to the bank, cashed the check, and made my $1,500 payment. I believe that God responded to my faith in a very unexpected way and that need was met. My belief is that whatever you're believing for in the future needs to transition to faith in the "NOW moment", and that is always and only demonstrated by corresponding action.

We have a tendency in the church to talk about what God is going to do in the future. It seems like it's always something like, "God's fixin' to do something big!" and not enough about the present moment. In John 4:35, Jesus confronted the habit of folks who always talk about what's coming, but never take it to the present moment. He said,

> "Do you not say, 'There are still four months and then comes the harvest'? Behold, I say to you, lift up your eyes and look at the fields, for they are already white for harvest!"

In effect, Jesus was saying, "The harvest is now! Quit putting it off!" I'm just as challenged by this word as you may be, so let's be wise, take action, and make the most of every opportunity, because the days are evil[3]. Bringing your faith into the NOW and taking action is a game changer that will give you a huge advantage over those who delay.

Biblically speaking, belief is evidenced by movement, not opinion or mere agreement. As James 2:17 put it, "Faith without works is dead". Faith keeps moving. It doesn't falter, it doesn't hesitate, and it doesn't stop. If you stop moving towards the goal that once burned bright in you, if you hesitate too long, not to catch your breath or wait on God for direction, but if you delay because you now doubt what you once believed – the vision, dream, or goal God gave you may pass on to someone else.

If you look at the context of Mark 9:23 you will find a father whose son was mute, and demon possessed. Jesus' disciples were unable to deliver the boy. When Jesus said all things were possible to him that believes, the father revealed an often-overlooked reality. He said, "Lord, I believe; help my unbelief." This demonstrates that belief is not necessarily an on off concept. It's layered.

We often say that we believe, and give an intellectual acknowledgement to its truth, but contradict it with things like fear, conflicting language, and even our subconscious identity. When Peter walked on water and then began to sink, Jesus asked him, "Why did you doubt?" Great question, now catch this...

The Greek word for doubt (*distazō*) means "to stand in two places". This is not about disbelief where you simply don't think something is possible or will happen. This is simply divided belief. As James 1:8 points out,

> "... he who doubts is like a wave of the sea driven and tossed by the wind. For let not that man suppose that he will receive anything from the Lord; A double minded man is unstable in all his ways."

In the Ultimate Success Framework referenced earlier (page 77), you learn that belief in the heart begins with INPUT (primarily what you watch and listen to), which leads to THINKING (consideration, meditation), which leads to SEEING (on the inside with the eyes of your understanding), which then drops down into your heart and becomes BELIEF. Your heart is the realm of your emotions, which are a good indicator of what you really believe. Your actions tell everyone else what you really believe.

Many believers are quick to say, "God is able", but have a hard time believing God will do it through them, or for them, or do it "now". James 2:19 is a stark reminder that "even the demons believe", and tremble. James goes on to make the case that our faith must also have movement (works) or it is dead (useless).

That brings me back to birds. How is it that they can leap off a high tree branch and fly so easily? Of course, they have wings, and it is their design, but it goes deeper. Birds are not struggling to believe that what they cannot see will support them. They're not trying to believe. They are simply unconflicted.

Romans 12:3 says that "God has dealt to each one a measure of faith". That means we've all been given some. Now, think of faith as a muscle. We've all been given muscles. We all have biceps and triceps, etc., but your muscles are far more developed than a newborn baby's muscles. Same number and same type of muscles. Yours are developed. Theirs are not yet.

According to 2 Thessalonians 1:3, faith grows. The nature of the faith God has given us is something that grows. Growth requires food and exercise. Feed on the Word of God. Let it move from input, to consideration, to imagination (seeing), to believing. Then practice what you believe in small actions because faith strengthens much like muscles do, through use, not analysis.

I remember when I started selling copiers in Nashville. I told God I wanted to succeed in that job, not because I wanted plaques or awards or recognition. I wanted to be a witness for Him, and I knew that folks are more interested in listening to someone they deem as successful than from someone who hasn't figured it out yet.

With that in mind, I asked God to help me set a goal that would blow their minds but be within what I was capable of believing. The company said they expected zero sales my first month and only two in my second month, and four a month thereafter. So, after praying I felt I could stretch for ten sales in my first full month on the job. I didn't sit in the office waiting for people to walk in and purchase. I did my part, prospecting, presenting, and closing sales.

On the last day of the month, I had eight sales, more than enough to stagger my peers and upper management, but with only three hours left on the last day of the month, I was still believing I would somehow get two more sales, despite having no more prospects to close. I detail this story in my ***Selling Among Wolves – Without Joining The Pack*** book, but suffice it to say, God sent one man by who purchased a copier and that triggered a prospect who had decided not to purchase to change his mind, and he bought as well, bringing my total to ten sales in my first full month.

My point in that story is that I wasn't strong enough in my faith to believe for twenty sales, or even eleven sales. For whatever reason, my faith latched on to a total of ten. It seems like a small thing now, but it was a big deal to me then. Faith is like that. It grows stronger with use.

Now, back to my question for you. What if you knew that you could not, indeed would not, fail? What if you knew that whatever venture you embarked on would ultimately succeed? Not necessarily without challenges, but in the end, it would succeed. What would you undertake? What "God dream" is inside of you? What vision have you written down? What stirs deeply within you?

When I talk about believing that you won't fail, I'm not suggesting passive faith where you don't cooperate with God and do the requisite work. It's a partnership where you work, and God blesses with favor, direction, wisdom, insight, etc. When birds leap off the branch, they always put action to their faith. They flap their wings, and only then, does the air they cannot see provide the support they must have.

I read about an interesting experiment where subjects were implanted with a small metal device in their brain, and were told it would enhance their capabilities. According to the testimony of one neuroscientist involved in this study, the device gave no special enhancements to the subject at all. Its purpose was to make the subject believe they had enhanced abilities that others didn't have. It was **that specific belief** that elevated their confidence, focus, and intuition.

We don't need a device implanted in our brain to enhance what we're capable of. We need the Word of God implanted or engrafted in our brain. James 1:21 uses that very language when it says,

> "Receive with meekness the engrafted word, which is able to save your souls."

Let me break this down for you. "Receive" here means to welcome into your mind like you would receive a guest into your home, giving it a place to stay. "With meekness" means to receive it in voluntary surrender.

Here's where it gets deep. "Engrafted" is an agricultural term where you take something living and graft it into living tissue. The idea here is that God's Word (which is living and powerful[4]) can be grafted into our inner life. It becomes part of us. But that doesn't happen by merely reading Scripture. Time and nourishment are required. You have to make a welcome place for it, then reinforce it by meditating on it, speaking it, and yes, acting on it. In so doing you are strengthening the neural pathways, so it becomes a living part of you.

"Which is able to save your souls" means that the engrafted word will progressively rescue, heal, and reorder your inner life until it reflects God's design. Your mind is a garden. What are you growing in it?

When I talk about whatever you step out to accomplish will succeed, it is based on Scriptures like Psalm 1:3, but conditional upon verse one and two...

> "Who walks not in the counsel of the wicked, nor chooses the path of sinners, or joins the company of mockers. Their delight is in the law of the Lord, in which they meditate day and night. Such a person will be like a tree planted beside the rivers of water, that produces fruit in season and whose leaves do not wither. That person is the one who will succeed in everything they undertake."

That promise in Psalm 1 is an echo of a promise God gave Joshua...

> "Only be strong and very courageous, that you may observe to do according to all the law which Moses My servant commanded you; do not turn from it to the right hand or to the left, that you may prosper wherever you go."

Even the apostle John prayed that...

> "you may prosper and be in health, even as your soul prospers"[6].

To be clear, the Bible doesn't promise blanket prosperity, but it does promise that aligned obedience with a well-ordered life will yield multiplied fruit. It's not hocus pocus. It's not what some people refer to as a prosperity gospel. It's just simple, fundamental truth. How much of that truth we walk in, is up to us. As Jesus repeatedly said,

> "Be it unto you as you have believed"[7].

In the Chapter Thirteen, I'm going to open up "Exhibit A" that Jesus taught that will challenge your assumptions about your identity because faith is less about what you believe God can do, or has done, and more about who you believe you are in relation to Him.

After all, sons and daughters trust differently than servants. Faith grows when you act from belonging, not when you act for approval.

References: Psalm 1:3 2) Mark 9:23 3) Ephesians 5:16 4) Hebrews 4:12 5) Joshua 1:8 6) 3 John 2 7) Matthew 8:13 and Matthew 9:29

CHAPTER 13

FAITH SECRETS OF BIRDS

What They Can Teach You if You Care to Learn

"Are you living your life like you are sparrow-priced?"

When people want to be inspired, or to be an inspiration, it's not uncommon to use the image of a lion, like MGM studios used to do at the beginning of all their movies. Lions, with their golden manes and proud walk, inspire a sense of awe, especially when you hear them roar. Similar to that, is the effect the image of an eagle has on people. Watching them soar or swoop down and catch a fish is awe inspiring. Horses are fast and oxen strong, but when Jesus wanted to inspire His disciples, He reached into His creation and offered the tiny sparrow as Exhibit A.

In Matthew 10, He says,

> "Are not two sparrows sold for a copper coin?... Yet not one of them will fall to the ground outside your Father's care... Fear not; therefore, you are of more value than many sparrows.[1]"

In that culture, 2000 years ago, sparrows were numerous, unglamorous, and very small. They were almost worthless, but would be caught, bundled together, and sold for food to the poorest buyers. The sparrow was anything but inspiring. But Jesus chose that little bird as an example of God's loving attention.

The sparrow lives as if it knows God's eye is on the sparrow. It builds its nest in humble settings, nothing auspicious about them. It forages throughout the day without a worry in the world and feels no need to hoard. It ends each day with no idea what tomorrow holds, has no clue about the weather forecast, and isn't guaranteed safety, yet if you watch them flit around by the outdoor café, it's as if it thinks the universe in which it lives was designed somehow for its personal existence.

We call that instinct, but that sounds mechanical, automated, as if the bird is some kind of windup toy. God observes their movements and makes sure their needs are attended to. What we call instinct in birds is really God's wisdom operating in them without resistance or intellectual argument. Birds don't analyze the promise of provision, they live instead with a constant knowing that provision is certain. Here's a big question for you...

Are you living your life like you are sparrow priced?

Not worth much, a dime a dozen, nothing special? Do you discount your value, lowball your work, cling to clients who demand much, but pay little, because you're afraid of what might happen if you lose them? And as a result, you don't have the time or bandwidth to find and serve clients at a much higher level. Your worth is not found in the market's appraisal or listed on your website.

You need only to know the Father's gaze
to realize your true worth.

We barely notice birds, but God not only feeds them daily, He also tracks their movements even though their market value is less than a penny. Have you considered that God tracks your life with much more interest than He does a sparrow? Won't He much more keep track of your monthly revenue, your career, and your next assignment?

The sparrow pulls the curtain back on a different economy where your confidence is not in how much you charge, but rather who is in charge of you.

It's not about your invoice, it's about your adoption,
by whom we cry, Abba! Father![2]

The deeper that truth lands, the less you are prone to worry and the more capacity you have to take bold and courageous action.

The Robin and the Myth of Perfect Conditions

As winter gives way to spring and the snow build up has melted into the lawns, making the ground soft and soggy, you'll find robins hopping across the terrain despite the damp chill still in the air. Not only are they often the first song you'll hear in the dawn chorus of the birds, but they are many times the first to forage after the weather has turned rough.

While other birds remain secluded in their safe place, waiting for the wind to die down and the sun to come back out, the robin is already on the field of play, probing the softened soil and pulling up worms that have crawled closer to the surface. It's not waiting for perfect conditions to unfold. The robin merely trusts what it knows to be true... the provision is waiting for it. From what I've observed...

Hesitation is the biggest dream killer.

Solomon warned...

"He who observes the wind will not sow, and he who regards the clouds will not reap"[3].

We justify our hesitation in a myriad of reasonable sounding justifications, but the one who demands to know the end from the beginning before launching out, never launches.

We say things like, "Our website needs to be redesigned", "We're working on the right pricing, the right marketing, the right messaging, the right timing...", etc. In the meantime, months or years pass by as we wait for that perfectly aligned timing that never comes. Offer after offer stays "in development", and we start planning the next thing instead, repeating the cycle.

The robin, on the other hand, doesn't wait for perfect conditions. It doesn't mind getting its feet muddy. It can handle the ridicule of other birds. It will sing before the fog has lifted, forage when the grass is still dripping, and bring in a haul for the kids in the nest before half the forest birds have left theirs. Don't wait for perfect conditions... If you do, you're probably too late. Hence the expression, "the early bird gets the worm!" The perfect conditions you're waiting for only exist in your imagination.

Faith is the ability to live with unanswered questions
You don't know everything, and you don't need to. That is the point of faith... Trust when you don't know the details.

God told Abram to leave the country he resided in and head to a land that He would show him later[4]. Can you imagine the conversation he had with Sarai? "Sweetheart, we're moving up north. Let's pack up and go." Sarai asks some reasonable questions... "Are you nuts? Did you have a big argument with Billy Bob? What brought this on and exactly where are we going?"

Abram would have had to respond with, "God spoke to me and promised to show me later where exactly He has in mind. I really don't know, but isn't this exciting! I love this!" There is no record of the actual conversation of course, but I'll bet it was interesting.

When you step out in faith at God's invitation, in less than perfect conditions with incomplete information, you can count on His provision. Wait until you have everything buttoned down, and you'll most likely miss your opportunity.

Robins thrive because they trust the system, the process, and the ways of God who made both the storm and the rainbow.

Do the same and you'll enter the market earlier, have small failures faster, adjust faster, iterate faster, succeed faster, and cash in on opportunities others consider too risky to try.

The Eagle and the Secret of Surrendered Strength

Watch an eagle soar above and it will captivate you. There is something majestic about an eagle when it catches a warm thermal column. Its wings lock as its body stills. With the slightest tilt of its wings, it catches the updraft of invisible warmer air, and it carries him higher and higher.

The eagle doesn't have to burn excessive fuel to gain altitude. It doesn't have to manhandle gravity or beat its wings furiously to rise. It waits for the invitation of the wind itself, slowly drifting upward, beckoning whosoever will to tap into its quiet strength. When the eagle senses the thermal, it leans in. There's no battle to catch it, no attempt to tame it. Nothing forced. Just finding, yielding, trusting, and receiving.

It mirrors what we read in Zechariah 4:6, "Not by might, nor by power, but by My Spirit, says the Lord." Sure, there is some effort involved, some energy expended, but the effort is about cooperation, not compulsion. The genius of the eagle, indeed its strategic advantage, is not in the strength of its powerful wings, but in its learned sensitivity to atmospheric changes that can benefit it.

That's foreign to many of us. We live like our only option is aggressive, ceaseless wing flapping. Look at your calendar. Do you pull twelve-hour days often? Do you feel like you're constantly striving, but never arriving? Do you live a lifestyle of hustle as though that were somehow good? Do you believe you should work until exhausted to prove to others that you're really putting in the effort, and that if you're not perpetually tired, you're not really giving it your best?

The eagle gives us a different model... What if the most important part of your day was time spent in what Psalm 91:1 calls the "secret place"? In this secret place, you commune with God, feed on His Word, and receive your directives for the day, including where the thermals are – those places or circumstances that help you rise with little or no effort.

Make part of your success strategy the practice of looking for, and being sensitive to, God's thermals for you, those hidden updrafts of unexpected favor, timing, and unforeseen opportunity. What if your daily strategy shifted from, "How can I work harder today?" to "Where is the wind right now?" The first question spawns anxiety, while the second one fosters intimacy. Jesus understood this and watched to see what the Father was doing, then emulated that in like manner[5].

In business terms, it might mean noticing when one of your offers or products gains traction and leaning into that instead of rigidly adhering to a predetermined agenda. It might mean paying attention to conversations where people's eyes light up (that's a thermal) and creating offers that ride that energy. For example, whenever I told people about this book you're now reading, they immediately wanted to get some copies. Based on the reception I've been getting and the high level of enthusiasm to incorporate these truths into their lives, I will be offering an in-depth course and hopefully, weekend retreats to help folks turn this learning into permanent life changing benefit.

Swallows and the Provision that Meets You in Motion

This one is really my style. Swallows show us trust while in motion. These babies seem to be trying to mimic perpetual motion. They don't stop for a drink of water; they skim the surface of a lake or stream with their beaks open and somehow manage to not choke on the inflow. When they get hungry, they don't land somewhere for a bite to eat, they snatch flying insects out of midair and feed while flying. They change direction on a dime to navigate wind gusts or eddies.

For swallows, life is lived on the move. Provision meets them in the air while in motion. We see this pattern echoed with Abram when told to go to a land he had never been to[4]. Jesus invited the disciples to follow Him long before He explained where they were going or what it would entail. Peter only learned that he could walk on water AFTER he stepped out of the boat.[6]

People tend to get this backwards. They wait for a fully funded budget, and all the market data to come in, before committing to stepping out. On the one hand it could be considered sensible. On the other hand, one might think they don't need God's help because they've got everything covered. That's for you to decide, but swallows move first, then experience the provision as they fly.

For you it may mean making sales calls with a script that doesn't yet feel totally comfortable. It may mean making a presentation before you have it fully polished. That's okay. It may mean launching out into a ministry with little more than a vision, a hope, and a prayer, trusting that God will provide the contacts and provision you need as you go.

Going swallow style is exhilarating, but it's not reckless. It doesn't mean foolishly signing contracts you haven't read and jumping into deals you haven't prayed and heard God about. You don't jump off the cliff and try to figure out what's next on the way down.

> Swallow style living is prayerful obedience expressed as courageous motion. It's the refusal to let unfinished details keep you sitting on the branch.

The Kingfisher's Courage

The kingfisher's survival depends on their willingness to dive headfirst into water at speeds approaching 60 mph to catch a fast moving, twitchy fish. But as you know from earlier in the book, water plays tricks on your eyes because light bends as it passes from air to liquid, so that objects are not where they appear to be.

Fortunately for the kingfisher, God designed them with the hardware to compensate for refraction and to adjust the angle of their attack midair, a split second before hitting the water. The water may have a ripple on it and be reflecting the dazzling sun back at it. There is uncertainty built into every dive, yet it still rolls the dice and takes the plunge. That's a lot like life.

For the kingfisher, the moment of highest trust is the instant just before its beak breaks the water. It has already committed and can't abort the mission. It must trust its instincts and believe it will get the fish or it will resurface hungry, because without taking that risk, there is no meal. Perhaps it's God's way of training us, but it seems that...

Provision often is only revealed at the point
of impact – not before you take the leap.

Don't be a Dodo Bird

The dodo bird lived in relative isolation on the island of Mauritius until its extinction in the late 1600's. On its isolated homeland, it had no predators and no fear when humans came and brought some animals that were predatory. It was brought to extinction due to its lack of awareness of the threats and its inaction when threats came their way.

Trust Empowers Action, It Doesn't Replace it

I cite the dodo bird to make the point that fearless trust is not naivety. Birds trust wisely, not foolishly. Sparrows still build nests. Robins do too, and they don't sit around waiting for God to throw some food in the nest. All birds forage. Geese still fly in formation to conserve energy and wrens still watch for predators.

The hallmark of true trust is not being less aware or less alert. Genuine trust will make you more alert. You will be more discerning about potential threats without being dominated by them. You will spot potential opportunities quicker and adapt quickly as needed, instead of being rendered useless by fear of failure. You will take wise precautions while refusing to get weak kneed about worst case scenarios. Don't be complacent and call it faith, and when it doesn't work out, blame God. In short, "Don't be a dodo!"

When was the last time you hesitated on an opportunity, and it passed you by? Was your hesitation more about fear than you care to admit? Was it less about being prudent and more about a lack of belief, not in the opportunity itself necessarily, but unbelief in God's willingness or ability to meet you on the other side of your "yes"?

The swallow's motion, the robin's early start, the kingfisher's dive, the eagle's surrender to wind, all of these offer blueprints for fearless execution. A swallow minded entrepreneur will start with the version they can build today, trusting that clarity and refinement will come while they are in motion. A robin like leader won't be moved by the storm, but will see it as an opportunity to get a head start.

An eagle hearted CEO will stop relentlessly expanding into every possible niche and instead ask, "Where is the Spirit clearly breathing on our work right now?" A kingfisher style decision maker will gather wise counsel, pray, then act decisively knowing that successful people make decisions quickly and rarely change them, while unsuccessful people make decisions slowly and change them often.

Faith based entrepreneurs consistently outperform fear based ones not because they are reckless or more talented, but because they trust God with the outcome enough to commit to the process. Trust generates action. Action generates lift. Lift generates momentum. Momentum makes space for breakthrough.

When Trust is Missing

What happens to you when trust is missing? It's more than just standing on the ledge a little longer. You morph into someone or something different. Something inside you begins to atrophy. Your "faith muscle" that once excited you now remains dormant, becoming weaker with every time you deny it the opportunity to obtain the precious promises God offers.

Lack of trust fosters anxiety and anxiety eats at your guts. It leaks into every conversation and is a contagion that affects others. In fact, it seeks others to infect or affect, as a way of building support and justification for its cowardice. Ouch! Anxiety causes paralysis and chronic indecision, bringing progress to a complete standstill.

Jesus told a parable where a man was given money to invest. Instead, due to distrust in his master's character, he buried the money and just returned it to his master upon his return. His distrust fed his fear. His fear led to inaction. Instead of gaining safety by doing nothing, he lost what he had.[7]

Don't be one who buries your gifts, talents, and opportunities in the name of "playing it safe" instead of trusting the heart of the One who gave you those gifts, talents, and opportunities in the first place.

Birds defy that deception every day. If a sparrow can leap off the telephone wire today, you can trust Him enough to pick up the phone and make that risky call, pursue that sales prospect, apply for the promotion or new job.

Why Birds Don't Worry

If you think about it, birds have a lot more to worry about than you. They live in the open in pretty basic nests. Not much shelter from the storm and no relief from the heat or cold. To keep them alive, their metabolism runs fast which means they have to eat frequently or perish. They have little margin for error, and a broken wing is a death sentence. They have predators that stalk them from above and below, they have fragile bones, and are exposed to threats every day.

You think that might make them a bit paranoid and live in a state of constant dread, but from every observation we can make, they live fully engaged in the moment, sometimes singing their heart out, other times busily foraging for food, courting, or taking a vacation (migration).

Worry is not in their makeup. It wasn't part
of our original makeup either, we had to learn it.

We arrive on the planet wired for trust, fearless and unafraid of snakes, spiders, and bees. We don't give a moment's thought to the mortgage payment or making sales. Over time and with experience, we make mistakes, encounter disappointments that teach us to hold back, to be cautious, even fearful. Culture tells us that we are the rainmakers and "If it is to be, it's up to me". There's always a kernel of truth in these things but the end result is we become experts at what to avoid and neophytes at trusting God.

Jesus points to the birds too numerous to miss, to help us unlearn what we've been conditioned to believe, and to confront our false assumptions. If God so faithfully sustains these fragile featherweight birds with such care, you can be certain He will sustain you and me with great care and love.

When you place your trust in God, you are not denying difficulty, you are putting your confidence in His much larger faithfulness.

Time to Leave The Nest

Every chick that once felt comfortable and safe from its condo in the treetops arrives at the time when the edge of the nest that kept it safe now becomes a ledge from which it must leap if it is ever to discover its potential and fulfill its purpose. The parent can demonstrate flying till the cows come home, but it cannot leap off the ledge for the young bird.

Just like you can't learn to ride a bicycle from watching a video, you will never learn to fly until you take that leap. No amount of information can stand in for the learning that comes from being the one to take the leap. The physics of flight cannot be mastered from the nest, any more than a trapeze artist can master tightrope walking from watching Nick Wallenda. Only in the air does the bird learn that its design holds, and it can fly.

Maybe you're standing on the edge of your comfortable nest. The leap you're contemplating may be something like, asking for her hand in marriage, or perhaps it's to launch the business idea you've had for a few years. Maybe it's time to close this chapter in your life and take on that new assignment that won't let go of your heart.

If the wind of God's Spirit is stirring you, and you know what has been etched on your heart and your natural abilities, then the question is not whether God can or will support you when you leap, but rather, will you trust Him enough to take the leap?

When you do finally jump, the initial ride will likely be pretty wobbly, much like the first time you tried to ride a bicycle. You may make a few mistakes, bump into a few things, knock some things over, but you will discover what every bird that has come into the world has always known... The One who created gravity also created lift!

You were crafted for adventure, for bold leaps and exploits. You were designed for Spirit led movement, surrendered effort, and the ability to access the provision He stored up for you in advance. You weren't made to rehearse what could go wrong. You were made to fly. The sky is calling. You are worth more than many sparrows.

It's time to leap
Without fearless trust, you will miss your purpose and destiny in life. More importantly, you will miss out on the most amazing relationship you can have with God Himself. With trust, you will go far, accomplish much, and be fulfilled.

But as powerful as trust is, it always brings the traveler home again. Every great journey leads back to the place where faith becomes form, and hope becomes your habitat, where what the heart believes becomes the world it builds.

In Chapter Fourteen, discover how birds craft the very environment that shapes their future and the destiny of their offspring,

References: 1) Matthew 10:29, 31 2) Romans 8:15 3) Ecclesiastes 11:4 4) Genesis 12:1 5) John 5:19 6) Matthew 14:29 7) Matthew 25:14-30

CHAPTER 14

CRAFTING YOUR ENVIRONMENT THAT SHAPES DESTINY

Nesting and Building

"You seldom rise higher than the world you construct around yourself."

We become what we are consistently immersed in. Our good intentions matter, but they do not shape us. The environment we remain in, trains us. As Solomon said...

> "He who walks with wise men will be wise, but the companion of fools will suffer harm[1]"

...which demonstrates that wisdom and foolishness are contagious. Paul reminds us that, "Bad company corrupts good morals."[2], which demonstrates that environment overpowers virtue when exposure is constant.

Birds show how environment affects outcomes. Many species must be immersed in the song of their fellow species members to learn to sing correctly. Those same birds, if raised apart from their natural environment, will develop a malformed song. If they are placed near a different species, they learn and adopt the song they are exposed to. That is why...

Training goes further with presence and
learning needs environment.

Birds instinctively understand the importance of creating the right environment. Before the robin pulling a worm from the earth ever had its first taste of success. Before it sang its first song. Well before those baby blue eggs were nestled beneath the mother robin's breast, or one of the hatchlings made its first trembling leap into the air saying under its breath, "I sure hope this works!", a marvel of engineering unfolds.

It is not reported on the news, nor does it gather any views or attention on social media. There is no monetization involved, no recognition or applause. But somewhere in the hollow of a tree or one of its sturdy branches, maybe in a hedge or on the face of a cliff, perhaps even in a cave or in an old barn, a bird begins to craft an environment that will train the next generation.

Depending on the species, it will gather a twig, then more twigs, perhaps a bottlecap, maybe some animal hair caught on a fence. It may use a scrap of grass, a piece of moss, even some spider silk if they can find it.

They take ordinary scraps and turn them into perfectly suited architecture for nurturing what they are called to raise. They do this quietly, without fanfare, attracting little notice. They are meticulous in the building of their nest because they know what is at stake. Nothing about their nest is haphazard.

The bird does not get bored one day and decide to try and build something like a child might do with a set of Legos. It is not experimenting. It is not trying to copy the latest nest building fad, nor does a robin in any way copy the architecture of a different species because maybe the weaverbird nest looks cool.

It is very deliberate in its attention to detail because
the future it's preparing for, demands preparation.

They live with the inner knowing that your environment shapes your destiny, and...

You seldom rise higher than the world
you construct around yourself.

Before a bird carries new life within, it carefully crafts a place that can safely hold that life. Before it ever lays on the eggs that will one day be a new generation, it creates a place of safety to ensure there will be a future for them. Before it takes on tomorrow's responsibility of rearing a brood of chicks, it meticulously structures today's reality.

When a bird builds a nest, it is more than a shelter from the elements. It is an expression of the vision they have received from God, and they know they must build. It is a preview of a future outcome that they know the future requires in order to be fulfilled. They are making a statement of expectation saying in effect, "This is what my calling requires. This is what those that come after me will rest upon and be nourished in." Success in life and business operates in much the same way.

Before results are generated or fruit appears,
there is always structure.

Before growth, there is always the environment in which growth occurs. Before breakthrough, there is always a nest. How you build your nest, and what that means for your future, is what this chapter is about.

The Hidden Genius Above Your Head

I have never been too impressed with the few bird nests I have seen. From the exterior, they look somewhat random. A few twigs, some grasses, fairly simple. But that is part of the plan. They are not supposed to look particularly grand from the outside. They are meant to blend into their environment and be less noticeable to predators.

The truth is, bird nests are marvels of engineering compressed into a few inches of space. They are miniature cathedrals of purpose, interwoven with nature's elements and oriented with surprising precision. Here, form follows function. Structure becomes a masterclass of survival, and every piece of material used serves the bigger vision of nurturing life above the vanity of appearance.

Imagine for a moment that you were dropped into the middle of a national forest, nowhere near any roads or stores. There is no Home Depot or Lowes nearby. You are getting cold and tired, and you need shelter. There is an extraction team coming to rescue you, but it will be six months before they arrive. All you have available to build your shelter with, is whatever you can find in the forest. You have no tools. You have no training. You have never built anything before. And one more thing...

You have no arms.
Welcome to bird life!

Despite those significant limitations, birds build their nests accounting for the angle of the branch and the strength of the prevailing wind. They position the entrance away from the driving rain and make accommodation for an emergency exit if needed.

They choose materials suitable for the climate, placing stronger, clunkier twigs on the outside and softer insulation like moss or grass on the inside. They top it all off with a camouflage outer layer of bark or similar materials so predators will not see it. They do all of that with no training, no tools, and no arms. If we built our homes with the same ratio of intelligence to brain size, our homes would make Trump Tower look like a housing project.

One of the more impressive examples of bird architecture is the Southern Masked Weaverbird. With that black mask he is wearing, he could earn the nickname "Zorro". This bird is remarkable and begins building its nest while hanging upside down near the end of a tree limb. Using long strands of grass and reeds, and nothing but its beak and the blueprint etched in its imagination, it ties the first loop tight enough to become the anchor of the entire structure.

Once that anchor is in place, it begins weaving more and more strands in overlapping spirals, creating a basket that can endure violent storms and support the weight of its growing family. Being security conscious, it places the entrance at the bottom of the dangling nest, making it difficult for snakes and other predators to gain access.

In the world of biomimicry, where science learns to imitate the wisdom of God displayed in creation, engineers have studied the structure of weaverbird nests, particularly the knots used to secure them, and applied those insights to the design of safer, more durable suspension bridges. The weaverbird had no formal education. It never attended a "do it yourself" home building seminar. It had no physical blueprint to analyze and guide it. It is simply putting on display one aspect of God's wisdom using the most rudimentary elements available.

God placed within the weaverbird the "know how" to build its nest, and it always builds that kind of nest. It is part of God's hardwired wisdom for that species. The weaverbird is not entering its nest into a science fair. It is not trying to get published in Architectural Digest. It is not competing with other birds. This is about legacy. The weaverbird instinctively understands that excellence in environment stimulates and supports excellence in outcomes. A poorly constructed nest leaves eggs vulnerable and legacy at risk. A strong nest secures the future.

When I considered the structures birds build and what motivates them to build with purpose, wisdom, and excellence, it led me to evaluate the structures in my own life. That includes habit structures, workspace structure, systems, and even relationship structures.

The quality of the structures I construct around my life shape the quality of what my life will produce. Building a sloppy nest with little regard for the future, and asking God to bless it, is a fool's errand. The grace of God does not bypass the need for sound architecture. It partners with it.

Legacy Nests

Speaking of legacy, when it comes to building nests, consider Mr. and Mrs. Eagle. They build high in a tree, starting with a basic platform of sticks, then adding to it year after year, one layer at a time. Eagle nests that began modestly have been known to reach as much as nine feet across, stand two stories high, and weigh as much as a small car. What the parents build is passed on to the next generation, and there are documented eagle nests that have been in continuous use for more than a century.

The message of the eagle's nest is simple and profound. Build with the future in mind. Not just your immediate future, but for those coming behind you. My mentor, Peter J. Daniels, designed his life with the intent to make an impact that would last three hundred years.

Each year, as the eagle adds another layer of branches, making the nest larger and more secure, it is in effect saying, "There is more life coming after we are gone, and we are preparing the way for their success."

Consider this... Scripture often refers to the God of Abraham, Isaac, and Jacob. These were not friends, partners, or brothers. God was telling a multigenerational story. King David wanted to build a house for the Lord, but God denied him that privilege because of the blood he had shed.

Instead, the construction of the temple was passed on to Solomon. Yet David spent years acquiring and setting aside gold, silver, bronze, iron, wood, and precious stones so that his son would begin with abundance rather than lack. David prepared for something he knew he would never live long enough to see begin, let alone finish.

When it comes to your professional and business life, who are you building for? Is it only for yourself, or are you also building with the next generation in mind, whether children, protégés, or team members?

Are you creating systems and structures that will outlive your involvement, or is everything dependent on you being present?

If what you are building cannot survive your departure, you're not building a nest. You're just collecting sticks.

Mud, Adaptation, and the Future

Swallows take a very different approach to nest building. Despite having no hands, they scoop wet mud with their beaks, mix it with their saliva, form it into small pellets, and press them against the underside of a bridge, the face of a cliff, or the beams of an old barn. They repeat this process again and again, shaping a bowl-like nest that hardens like clay fired in a kiln. Once complete, the nest becomes remarkably durable, capable of withstanding weather, vibration, and time.

They build so discreetly that to the casual observer; the nest appears to be part of the structure itself. If a home is later built nearby, they may relocate and rebuild near an outdoor porch light. When their environment changes due to construction or human encroachment, they adapt. Life works the same way. God's call on your life does not change with the times, but the way you carry it often must.

Sometimes a new season requires a new nest.

Hummingbirds, themselves masterpieces of engineering, build nests that reflect their uniqueness. The female gathers plant fibers and spider silk, weaving them together into a structure that is both strong and elastic. As the chicks grow, the silk stretches, allowing the nest to expand without compromising its integrity. She builds with future growth in mind.

Many people build their lives with only the next payment in view, or the next customer through the door, or the next deal to close. They design a life that cannot properly accommodate growth. When new opportunities arrive, quality declines, relationships strain, reputations suffer, and the business contracts in response.

Build with growth in mind. Think in terms of scalability. Develop a mindset that welcomes expansion and plans for it, rather than fearing growth and unconsciously resisting it. The hummingbird nest is both beautiful and functional. Both can exist in your life as well. You can be productive and peaceful, surrounded by beauty, without sacrificing efficiency. Whether it is an osprey nest perched high atop a power pole or a robin's nest hidden among the branches of a cherry tree, the structures birds build, reflect God's wisdom embedded deep within their design. They do not improvise away from that wisdom. They do not deviate.

The nests they build are not only to meet their own needs, but to serve as living demonstrations of God's wisdom for our benefit. This is why Jesus instructed us to consider the birds. How much consideration you give them is up to you, but even a lifetime of study would barely scratch the surface of what they reveal. The more you learn, the more you realize how much wisdom remains to be discovered.

Consider this. Before God placed Adam in Eden, He planted a garden. Before Israel entered the Promised Land, God promised wells they did not dig and houses they did not build. Before Jesus sent out His disciples, He immersed them in years of close proximity, teaching, and spiritual atmosphere. Before He welcomes us into eternity, He promises, "I go to prepare a place for you."[3]

If God considers preparation and environment important enough to build into every living creature, and if He prepares landing places for us both in life and beyond, then perhaps we should do the same. I believe it only makes sense that we should give serious thought to the nests we build to accommodate what He wants to release through our lives.

The Nest in Your Mind

The nest of your mind is the place where ideas are laid instead of eggs. It is where they are nurtured, fed, and developed. If your mind nest is filled with negativity, those ideas have little chance of survival and almost no chance of success. Even the quality of the ideas you place there will be compromised if the nutrients that formed them were questionable, infused with insecurity, fear, or poor information.

If you want to build a strong, stable, and secure mind nest, you must intentionally structure the environment for greatness. Paul refers to this as the renewing of the mind. Renewing always begins by first tearing down structures, habits, and patterns that do not align with the future you are called toward. This includes things like mindless scrolling, constant exposure to media that fuels anger, lust, outrage, complacency, or trivial distraction.

We become like what we consistently feed on

If what you are consuming contradicts where you are going, it is time to let it go. Replace those inputs with material that prepares you for the purpose you were created to fulfill. If your calling is to be a great mother and raise strong children with a sense of destiny, then feed your mind with wisdom that equips you to do that well. If your calling is in business, study the biographies of leaders who have gone before you. Read the work of those who have succeeded in the arena you are stepping into, and learn from their experience.

The input you consume is the building material of your future. Build your mind nest with eternal truths. This obviously includes Scripture, but it also includes truths revealed through the things God has made. As Paul wrote in Romans 1:20, the invisible attributes of God are clearly seen, being understood by what He has created, even His eternal power and divine nature. When you invest intentionally in your mind nest, you are setting the table for success. You are preparing an environment from which future breakthroughs can launch, rather than hoping they appear in a hostile or neglected landscape.

Family Nests

Long before a child ever announces they are moving out or chooses their own path forward, they live in the family nest. Whatever they come to know about love and work, God and risk, conflict and consequences, they learn first in the environment you have built for them. What they need, to succeed in life, is not luxury or opulence. They need love, peace, and security. They need order and spiritual connection. They need boundaries that provide predictability and grace that helps them survive inevitable failures.

Build a family nest with shared meals and shared direction. Not at the granular level of micromanagement, but at the aspirational level of virtue, faith, and purpose. Have meaningful conversations. Let them hear the sound of spoken prayer. Teach them how to talk to God and how to listen.

Birds understand the basics of nest stewardship. They do not build on broken branches where instability could cause the eggs to roll out. They do not tolerate parasites. They remove them when discovered. They fix leaks. They repair, reinforce, and guard the structure.

The family nest works the same way. Parents must be willing to remove what harms, repair what is weakened, and reinforce what matters most. Declutter a child's bedroom (the nest within the nest) to give them a sense of order. Then require them to maintain it, not as punishment, but as preparation for greater responsibility.

Generally speaking, blessing flows through order.

When a child learns structure, they gain the confidence to build upon it. Teach them how to handle conflict instead of storing resentment. Teach them responsibility without shame. Above all, teach them about God. Lead them in prayer. Read Scripture with them. The family nest is not perfect, but it should be purposeful.

Business Nests

Nests provide structure and predictability. In business, structure shows up as systems and processes that move value from idea to execution. These include standard operating procedures, systems that guide raw material to finished product, service promised to service delivered, and people managed with clarity and care.

Every business must do three things well.
Create value. Sell the value. Deliver the value.

The more simply and smoothly those three functions operate, the stronger and faster the business will grow.

The nesting concept also applies to the environment in which you work. Does it inspire you or distract you? Have you designed it for creativity and efficiency, or do you operate in constant randomness? Consider your corporate culture. What tone do you set? What tone do you allow? How does that atmosphere contribute to your results?

In life and business, habits, patterns, relationships, and even the spiritual atmosphere you cultivate may seem small compared to the dream burning in your heart. Yet those very elements are the twigs, moss, and fibers of your destiny.

Legacy is not built in a day. It is constructed gradually, step by step, choice by choice. We are called to build for something larger than today, to build with a future in mind that may well outlive us. Build purposefully. Build intentionally. Build in ways that inspire. Build high enough for vision to remain clear. Build strong enough to endure inevitable storms.

Build beautifully, not for vanity, but to remind
your soul daily of God's nearness and care.

One day, when your children, your team, or those you serve catch the wind you have been preparing them for and take flight, others will notice. More importantly, God will say, "Well done, good and faithful servant,"[4] not only for the impact you made, but for the nest you built that made it possible.

Build well.

It's true that God instructs us to build wisely and create environments where destiny can be discovered, purpose can flourish, and lives can be strengthened, but building the nest is not the whole story.

We live in a world of seasons. As Scripture teaches in Ecclesiastes 3,

> "To everything there is a season, a God appointed time for every purpose under heaven."

In every life, there comes a season not to build, but to release. A time to loosen what once fit well, to lay down what carried you faithfully for a season but no longer aligns with the future God is unfolding.

Every bird understands this rhythm instinctively. No nest is meant to be permanent. Feathers wear. Branches weaken. Seasons shift.

What once provided safety can eventually become
confinement if it is clung to beyond its time.

We however, often struggle here. We hold on to old structures out of fear. Fear of loss. Fear of instability. Fear that letting go means starting over. Yet the same God who teaches us to build, also teaches us when to release.

Renewal is not abandonment.
It is obedience to timing.

A nest that once protected life must eventually be left behind so life can expand. If the bird never releases the nest, flight never matures. Potential remains unrealized. Destiny stalls.

There comes a moment when what once felt like shelter begins to feel restrictive. What once felt like safety begins to feel heavy. That discomfort is not failure. It is often the signal of transition.

This is where many people hesitate. They mistake familiarity for faithfulness. They confuse staying put with endurance. But endurance is not about refusing to move when God is clearly calling forward. Every bird must eventually leave the nest it worked so carefully to build. Not because the nest was wrong, but because the season has changed.

And so it is with us.

There are times when God calls you to step out of roles, routines, relationships, or responsibilities that once served you well. Not because they were mistakes, but because they have fulfilled their purpose. To cling to them is to resist growth. To release them is to cooperate with renewal. The same wisdom that teaches you how to build must also teach you how to let go.

That next season, the season of renewal, shedding, and preparation, is not about destruction. It is about alignment. It is about making room for what is coming by releasing what has already done its work.

And that is where we are headed next.

In the following chapter, we step into the sacred rhythm of renewal. You will discover why every bird must eventually release what it has outgrown, what that process looks like in real life, and how letting go is often the doorway to greater freedom, strength, and flight.

Turn to Chapter Fifteen... A new season is calling.

References: 1) Proverbs 13:20 2) 1 Corinthians 15:33 3) John 14:2 4) Matthew 25:21

CHAPTER 15

SHEDDING WHAT NO LONGER SERVCES

Molting And Renewal Cycles

"There comes a time where the old structure that supports, must be replaced, not repainted."

Have you ever felt like your life was going through an unplanned and perhaps unwelcome transition, where what seemed to be going fine was no longer working? Well, you're not alone. In the life of birds, that is a normal part of life, and there is no escaping it. Unlike birds, people usually resist it because they don't recognize it for what it is. It's called molting.

In every bird's life, there comes a season where they seem to have lost their luster. When birds are going through this process, you may notice their feathers sticking out at odd angles. Perhaps their tail feathers are uneven, and in the one I saw up close, its wings looked a bit ragged. Sometimes their color gets dull and patchy. The ducks in the lake across the street from my home spend more time ducking out of view in the reeds (pun intended) because for a short season, they can't lift themselves out of the water. Songbirds are equally bashful, but in a different way. They spend more time in hedges (for safety) than perched on open branches.

This isn't a plague. There's been no surge in predatory activity. It's just a temporary season called "molting," and it's not particularly comfortable as they find themselves in this awkward place between the bird they were and the bird they are becoming. In this season, they will shed the very feathers that carried it through storms and skirmishes, migration, and courtship. The very feathers that once served them well are too worn to adequately serve its future.

It may look to the casual observer that the bird is weak, but in fact it is going through a transition requiring more strength and courage than most people are willing to summon. The choice to let go of what no longer serves its destiny.

The Divine Reset System

This molting season is not a cosmetic upgrade, a little feather maintenance here and a little beak sharpening there. It is a total makeover, a full upgrade, a complete renewal cycle built into the biology of birds. As amazing as feathers are, they are somewhat fragile. Winds tear at them, rain beats down on them, the sun bleaches them, battles for the fairer sex take their toll, predators might get a piece of them, even branches can snag them. It gets to a point where some routine maintenance, aka preening, is not enough.

> There comes a time where the old structure that supported it, must be replaced, not just repainted.

Here's where it gets interesting. God arranges the time of molting. They don't choose it. It begins when the old feathers that worked so well, loosen up at the root and fall away, allowing new "pinfeathers" to push through the skin to replace them. It's important to understand that not every species molts at the same time, or at the same frequency, or even in the same way, but all species do molt.

During this time the bird may look pretty shabby, like it's a homeless, unkept bird due to the gaps in its plumage, which also makes it more vulnerable, hence the reason it lays low to avoid predators that it can no longer easily escape from. In some cases, flight is temporarily impossible. It's a difficult and vulnerable season for them, but they never opt out. They yield to the plan of God hardwired into their biology to shed, rest, and regrow.

The same cycle happens to all. Most don't recognize God's working in the process, and fight it. This chapter will help you through it. We were never meant to carry the same habits, structures, and beliefs through every stage of life. As I've matured in life, things I believed about God that may have helped me along no longer serve me in the same way. In Scripture there is the "milk of the word"[1], the "bread of the word"[2], and the "meat of the word"[3]. Like babies needing milk, there comes a time when we lay that aside for bread and meat.

The world in which we live is in constant change, and as it does, your assignment will likely shift as well. You may be called into a life of full-time ministry, but the way you walk that out will likely go through a number of iterations. Your body, your relationships, your surroundings, and market changes will all change as you move through seasons in your life. If you cling to what was, old ways, old identities, old strategies, you will find them strangely ineffective, and will experience what every bird does before the molting is complete: less lift, more drag, and more effort for less altitude.

Molting is God's way of taking you out of the field of play for a short season. He's not finished with you. Your race is not finished. He has a future with hope planned for you[4], but you can't run tomorrow's race with yesterday's feathers. David had a peek into this mystery when he wrote,

> "He satisfies your mouth with good things so that your youth is renewed like the eagle's"[5]

The eagle, like David and Isaiah claimed, does renew its youth, but the Biblical pattern of renewal, and what is demonstrated in eagles, is NOT one of self-destruction. Their beak and talons are scraped and flake off naturally through use. Their feathers are replaced incrementally and seasonally without interrupting flight, and it can take up to 2 years to replace all its feathers.

God's renewal program comes from alignment with the rhythms He has instituted, not from beating oneself up. He keeps inviting us to forsake old cycles and old habits that perhaps God overlooked in our ignorance[6], but He expects you to grow in your thinking and choose a different direction. For this He provides increased revelations of His grace, deeper revelation of His love, and greater capacity to embrace His higher calling for you.

In the New Testament, we are repeatedly instructed to "put off the old man, and put on the new man"[7]. That choice requires no self-flagellation. It's not a call to clean up our old nature. We let it go by embracing the new. In life that renewal process is not usually a single mountaintop experience. It comes in waves, is usually awkward and uncomfortable, but always tied to purpose.

Sometimes that means letting go of ways of thinking, how you perceive yourself, how you understand God, and related behaviors that all felt so right when you began, but no longer seem to fit with where you're going. It means embracing what may feel unfamiliar and uncomfortable but is equipping you for the upgraded role that He has prepared for you. Birds accept this as part of life. We tend to resist it until we have no other choice.

Four Molting Strategies

Birds like geese, ducks, and swans complete their molting in a short window, leaving them temporarily flightless. The feathers they're leaving behind would not make it through another migration, so God parks them on the sideline while they grow a new wingsuit.

Sound familiar?

Do you remember when things were moving along pretty smoothly? Maybe you were speaking at events, writing blogs, engaged in sales, running a successful startup, always creating something new, launching or testing a new idea, and then something shifted. Not obvious at first, but the season was shifting. The time for that was over. Maybe a health issue ushered in the change. Maybe open doors were suddenly closed. The role that felt so right for you, no longer feels like home. You're doing less, accomplishing less, traveling less, and it may be attacking your sense of identity and purpose.

If you get this wrong by thinking of it as failure on your part, you will most likely double down and try to get back in the game at the position you were playing, but that is like taping duct tape on a broken wing. It may hold, but it won't get you back to where you were, nor will it get you where your destiny is calling.

The lesson from the waterfowl is that being grounded from flying, is only for a season, and always with a purpose to quietly develop new and stronger capacity. During this season, your client base may thin, your sales may slow, your old relationships may drift away, but this is creating opportunity for new "pinfeathers" to push their way out with fresh wisdom, honed character, clearer strategy, and renewed spiritual authority.

Instead of fussing at God and arguing for your old life back, embrace the change and use the freed-up time to learn new things, acquire new skills, forge new relationships, develop new habits, and deepen your walk with God, so you'll be stronger, wiser, and ready for the next migration.

Inch by Inch, Anything's a Cinch

Those melodic songbirds we have come to love hearing, cannot afford to be flightless for weeks on end. Too many predators, and too fragile a body. Their process is different from a goose or duck. They molt gradually, shedding just a few feathers at a time, replacing them, and then continuing the process until all have been replaced. In a sense, they're always in a mode of transition, but rarely do they find themselves incapacitated, and if they are, it's for a very short time.

Some people live like that. They live in a constant state of renewal instead of a dramatic "turn your world upside-down" reboot. People who exhibit this tend to be learners. They constantly want to learn and grow. As they study or experience new things, some of the old falls off. Scripture has a way of doing that. The more time you spend marinating your mind in God's word, the more it is renewed. You might not notice the changes happening in you, but they are real and lasting. Others will probably see the change in you before you do.

Vincent Van Gogh stated,

> "Great things are not done by impulse,
> but by a series of small things brought together."

As James Clear, author of "Atomic Habits" put it,

> "All big things come from small beginnings.
> The seed of every habit is a single, tiny decision."

"Songbird renewal" works that way. One feather at a time. As each one is released and a new one grows in, you become more proactive and less reactive, your thinking sharpens, your goals are refined, your vision sharpens, your work becomes more focused, and your leadership becomes a force for good.

The way "songbird renewal" works in business is, instead of closing it down and starting over, you "molt" individual pieces or structures one at a time. For example, maybe you rewrite your sales page on the website, tweak your customer onboarding process, modify your follow-up procedures in your selling process, upgrade your software, etc. Nothing too drastic that could cripple your company if one of the changes failed, but taken together, over time, your company will fly higher and more efficiently, not because of one monumental pivot, but because of a dozen smaller molts that barely caught any attention.

The Catastrophic Molt

This is practiced by Emperor Penguins who live in the Antarctic. They shed almost all their feathers in an abbreviated period, and quickly grow a fresh set. During that time, they can't get in the water to feed because they are not waterproofed. They stand in the freezing cold, bunched up against each other for any chance of warmth, and remain like that, burning stored up fat until the new coat is complete. It seems kind of brutal but is necessary given the hostile environment they live in. Half measures would be deadly.

A catastrophic molt for a person might be a failed marriage, a business collapse, a church split, a financial disaster that removes the security of what you always counted on. It happens fast, almost overnight. Maybe you have some "stored fat" to last you for a while, but that usually burns quicker than you think it would.

Nothing feels right. Nothing feels familiar. Your roles change, your relationships with some are forever altered. Nothing is as it was, and the future you were once looking forward to has faded out of view.

Catastrophic molts are not God's "go to" strategy for course correction, but in His mercy, when gentle nudges and previous wise counsel were ignored, or when choices you previously made went horribly wrong, His grace is still extended to you.

During this time of molting, your theology becomes less theoretical and more experienced. Your judgment of others becomes compassion. You become equipped for an environment that once was off limits. What intimidated you in the past is only a shadow, and what drove you forward before, no longer entices. Behold, all things become new.

Then there's the Ptarmigan

Whose idea was it to spell it like that? Shouldn't it just start with the letter "T"? This bird lives in the arctic regions of the world, evidently preferring a spartan environment of tundra and snow. But this one, molts twice a year. In the summer it dons an attractive coat of mottled brown and gray feathers that blend perfectly with the lichen, moss, and stones. In the winter, it changes feathers and develops a strikingly attractive coat of pure white feathers, camouflaging them effectively in the snow from predators.

The simple lesson here is to adjust (not compromise) to changing environments and culture shifts. Don't go to market with last year's trends. Methods that worked in a previous season don't do so well now. Principles don't change, but strategies need to. Sometimes God will change your emphasis, but not your mission. What environment has God placed you in now? The Apostle Paul recognized the need to shift his messaging to accommodate the environment he was in, while keeping his mission, saying (in effect) that he molted by becoming "all things to all men," that he "might by all means save some"[8].

No Man's Land

Molting to me is a bit like fasting. It feels great when it's over, but the process is no fun. It's humbling. People don't see you the same way. The image you always projected of confidence, competence, and having it together yields to something uncomfortably vulnerable. During that season, we tend to withdraw if we can, or flat out deny what's happening and fake it, like all is well. Truth is, we don't really understand what is happening. We only know we're losing feathers.

Birds are free from the pressure to maintain an image. They know that their less than "put together appearance" is both necessary and temporary. The awkwardness they feel not being able to fly as high or as well or as far, is something they know will pass. And it does. It always does.

For you, it may mean telling clients that you're refining your product or service offerings. You may need to tell your friends that you're going through a season where you need to rethink what's next. You may even need to tell the Lord that you have no clue what's going on with you and ask for His help.

None of this means you're failing.
You're just learning how to process your molting.

When I went through a self-inflicted catastrophic molting in 1982, during which I shed everything but the clothes on my back, I repeatedly called out to the Lord and simply said, "Please don't let go of me." I was in a very difficult spot and didn't know the way out. All I knew for sure about God in that season was that I needed Him more than I needed my next breath. True to His character, He never let go of me. He was never going to.

Scripture offers this insight:

> "Though our outer man is wasting away, our inner man is being renewed day by day".[9]

Rest assured, on the outside your life might be in shambles, but on the inside, if you have let Christ in your heart, something stronger and more radiant is coming to life, and God who is faithful will complete the work He began in you.[10]

The Process

When we look at God's wisdom as built into molting, combined with Scripture, a clear process for personal "molting" comes into view.

First is recognition. Birds don't need to be told by anyone else that their feathers are beyond repair. They pay attention to their own wellbeing and know when to act. Where in your life does it feel like you're not getting lift like you used to? Where does it feel like the oil that once greased the skids, has dried up? Another way of asking that is, where do you sense the pleasure or grace of God for what you're doing has lifted? You've faced difficult things in the past, but this is different. These are signals of worn or damaged feathers.

Next is release. Before you can grow new feathers, you've got to let the old ones go. Maybe that's a succession plan in your business. Maybe it's releasing a relationship. I've said for a long time that you can't get to second base with one foot on first base. What is it time to let go of? Multiplication often begins with subtraction.

Then comes rest. This is not the time to double your workload in an effort to blunt the pain of change or avoid facing what God is wanting you to let go of. You may need some time off, or shorter workdays allowing extended time in the secret place that Psalm 91 speaks of, feeding on His word, meditating on His promises, and listening for His guidance.

After rest comes rebuild. You see a new path forward. It will require new habits, new roles, new structures, all of which may feel awkward at first, but like a new pair of boots, they will, with use, come to feel perfect for you as you step into the new season and align with the Spirit.

Finally comes reemergence. The struggle is over. The new direction is working. What you thought might never return has come back stronger and more fruitful with greater ease. Resilience increases. Momentum builds. Life is looking awfully good again. People will think you've made a comeback, and you have, but it was all part of the molting process that God brings all of us through. Different ways of molting for different people, but God is the author of it all.

A molting season is part of life. Everyone goes through it, usually more than once, but not everyone acknowledges it. Instead of surrendering to it, they choose low living with what they perceive to be predictable outcomes.

You may be in a season of molting right now. It could be a molting of relationships or a spiritual molting where things you once believed or didn't believe now change. It could be a molting in your career or business life. Don't give in to the temptation to judge yourself in this awkward middle. Trust God, knowing He is growing new wings in you.

Just like our corruptible body must put on incorruption, and our mortal selves must put on immortality to enter the hereafter[11], you're never going to step into the life God has for you wearing yesterday's worn-out feathers. But we serve a God who delights in renewal.

He was not caught off guard by the changes in your life, even the ones you regret. If you decide now to let go of what no longer serves, accept God's invitation to rest, and cooperate with the new thing He is growing in you, mark my words, there will come a day when you run toward the edge of your next season and leap.

When you do, you will discover that He is still there to carry you by the Spirit (that you still cannot see), higher than you have ever flown before. Not in spite of the molting season you endured, but because of it. Letting go is essential for growth. The old adage is still true: "Let go and let God."

Sometimes what we need to let go of, is the need for certainty. In this next chapter I share three unbelievable, but true stories, where I let go of my requirement for answers in advance, trusting I would find them as I went. They were like mini-migrations. Maybe you can relate?

References: 1) 1 Peter 2:2 2) John 6:35 3) Hebrews 5:12 4) Jeremiah 29:11. 5) Psalm 103:5. 6) Acts 17:30 7) Ephesians 4:22-24 8) 1 Corinthians 9:22 9) 2 Corinthians 4:16 10) Philippians 1:6 11) 1 Corinthians 15:53-54

CHAPTER 16

PERSONAL MIGRATION

Three Incredible Journeys That Shaped My Destiny

"It's the summons of silence, the magnetic pull of distance, an inner longing for a place they have never been but somehow remember."

Shortly after sunset, when temperatures are cooler and the air more stable, the sky becomes a blanket of black velvet with innumerable diamond-like stars glittering in the heavens. The frogs still croak, and the reeds still whisper in the stillness of the marsh as the mist settles in for the night, scattering the rising moonlight across the expanse. But this night is different…

Close to water's edge, in the midst of motionless bulrushes, a solitary bird cocks its head as if it heard something afar off that you missed. There is scarcely a breeze. No predators have arrived. No storm threatens on the horizon. Yet it looks into the heavens as if seeking confirmation. Something has shifted that defies observation.

The bird's heart begins to beat a little faster in anticipation. Its eyes scan the sky and the surrounding marsh to see if any other has picked up on the inaudible, untraceable signal. Its wings allow a subtle shimmer to pass from one end to the other, as if it were somehow going through a preflight checklist… or was it destiny itself brushing against its feathers? Whatever it is sensing, it cannot define, but it grows inexplicably restless, stirring, pacing. This insistent restlessness intensifies. It feels both holy and familiar.

Then, as if an angel were walking through the marsh awakening them to something big, more birds begin to stir and grow restless. They feel it in their bones. It traces through their feathers. It's the summons of silence, the magnetic pull of distance, an inner longing for a place they have never been, but somehow remember. How is that possible?

It reminds me of the saints of the Old Testament who, knowing they were but strangers and pilgrims on this earth, were looking for a heavenly home they hadn't seen, but knew was there. As Hebrews 13:14 puts it,

> "For here we have no continuing city, but we seek the one to come."

In the marsh where the stirring began, no older bird calls for a meeting to give instructions. None are needed. No senior bird unfurls a map of the world or draws one in the mud. There is no whiteboard, no planning meeting, no handing out of GPS coordinates. Collectively, they just know. The first bird leans into the gentle breeze, extends its wings, gives it a few wingbeats until lift exceeds drag, and the beautiful, invisible air catches it.

In that moment, a bird weighing less than a first-class letter becomes a traveler of the night sky, a pilgrim beginning a journey of thousands of miles, guided only by a compass it cannot read and a desire for a destination it, at best, has only heard of, both placed there by God deep inside its slender body, taking up no space, yet filling it with expectation.

Migration has begun.

This is not some random flight of fancy. It is not moving over to an upscale marsh out in the country it heard some ducks quacking about. This is obedience to something it cannot explain, nor does it understand. It just chooses to obey. It knows to trust the inaudible whisper it heard, and to believe that the wind that gives it lift will carry it all the way to its home away from home. It knows to trust its feathers, wings, and body structure, its untested ability to follow the unseen paths of God. This flight begins with a single "yes." So does every great journey of your life.

I suspect that most of us have had the urge to migrate. We've felt the tug. We heard something in the silence, inaudible, but unmistakable. But most of us wanted more certainty. We wanted to count the cost, to have the map, to know our stopping points, to understand the purpose… We wanted it all to make sense not only to us, but to others who would see us off on our journey. But it rarely does.

I've had three significant "migratory" experiences in my life, where I said "yes" to something I did not understand and could not explain. I share them here in the hope that it will give you courage to follow your next migratory call from God…

The Toronto Migration

I was born in Toronto at a very early age. Things weren't particularly stable at that time, and when I was three, my mother dropped me off at someone's doorstep. My father remarried his first wife, with whom he had three children, and I was the unwelcome "love child" in my new family. That marriage lasted about seven years, and when I was eleven, I was dropped off at my grandmother's apartment – never to see the only siblings I knew again – until…

I was twenty-five, living near Vancouver, British Columbia, with a successful career as a young sales manager in the copier business. For no apparent reason, I had an inexplicable and unshakeable urge to go to Toronto. It pressed upon me, but I knew no one there and had no reason to go. My siblings and stepmom lived there, but I hadn't seen them since I was eleven, and had no thought of trying to find them.

I grew restless on the inside. I had to fly back east to Toronto, but there was zero justification for it. After a week or so, I booked a flight and arrived in Toronto on a Wednesday night. Having no idea why I was there, I drove to the Airport Holiday Inn and got a room for the night.

The next day was cold and sunny. There were still small deposits of snow in places that got little sun exposure. With nothing else to do, I decided to drive 75 miles north to Lake Simcoe, where I spent my childhood summers in the early sixties. Of course, the last time I was there, I was in the back seat of a station wagon and the road to our cottage was all gravel.

Now, fourteen years later, nothing looked the same. The roads were paved, new development had come in, and after driving on the road that paralleled the lake (but not within sight of it) expecting to see something familiar, I got frustrated, pulled the car over, and got out to look around. The area I pulled over in was undeveloped, with ranch land on one side and woods on the other.

I was about to give up and head back to Toronto when my eyes caught something in the woods to my left. It was an old handmade, weather-beaten sign about the size of a license plate, with four rather faded letters painted on it. It simply read… P I N K. I had unwittingly stopped in front of the old property line. The cottage we spent summers in was not visible from the road, but from there I knew how to get to the road that had the driveway to the cottage.

The cottage was still boarded up for the winter and wasn't much to look at. The lake was still frozen over and offered nothing comforting to behold. My look around lasted less than five minutes. But the neighboring cottage had someone in it. The lights were on, and the woman inside was feeling poorly and had called her husband to leave work and take her to the doctor.

He arrived just as I was getting to my car, and I asked him if he knew who owned the boarded-up cottage now. He gruffly replied that his mother owned it. I asked her last name, and he said, "PINK." In somewhat of a shock, I said, "You must be David! I'm Michael!"

He was the oldest of my stepbrothers, nearly eight years my senior. He hugged me excitedly and invited me into the cottage next door, where he lived with his wife. He told me that he was so overwhelmed with the question of whatever happened to me, that on his way home from work the day before, as my plane was in the sky, he stepped into a random church to say a prayer for me. Prior to that, he only attended church to get married.

He and I were both amazed, me more than he, because I knew that I had come in response to an urge I didn't understand and couldn't justify. He quickly called his mother (my stepmom) and said, "Mom… guess who's here!" Without hesitation she replied, "Michael." How in the world could she have possibly known? Turned out that on her way home from work, she too had been similarly overwhelmed with whatever happened to me, and also stopped at a church on her way home to say a prayer for me, while my plane was still in the sky.

It gets wilder…

We agreed that we would all have dinner at her house on Saturday. Of my three siblings, one had taken his life about seven years earlier, so dinner was with my stepsister and David and my stepmom. It was there that I learned for the first time that I had another stepbrother. Apparently, my birth mother had a son who was six years older than me, but we were separated when I was so young that I grew up not knowing about him.

I found out his last name and the next day began to track him down, and to hopefully find my birth mother. The night before I was scheduled to fly back to Vancouver, I learned that my birth mother, who I thought I would meet, had died many years earlier, but I also finally learned where my newly discovered half-brother Kevin worked.

As I was packing to leave and catch my flight, I called what I was told was his employer. To my disappointment, they informed me that he had left the company about a year earlier, so I asked to speak with anyone who knew him from that time period. I was put through to someone I'll call Mary, and asked if she knew Kevin's whereabouts. Sadly, she told me no one had heard from him since his departure a year earlier. I left her the hotel phone number and said, "If you think of anything before I leave in the next hour, please call me back."

Amazingly, while Mary and I were speaking, Kevin was in another part of Toronto talking to a client who asked him if he could recommend anyone for a job position that he wanted to fill. Kevin thought about it for a minute and said, "Yes! There's a woman I worked with at Maclean's Magazine a year ago. Her name is Mary. I'll call her now."

Within about ten minutes of me hanging up from Mary, the hotel phone in my room rang, and it was my long-lost brother Kevin, who I hadn't seen since I was a toddler. He asked me to change my flight reservations because he was getting married in a couple days and he wanted me to meet his fiancé and attend his wedding.

When we were able to swap stories, he told me that on the previous Wednesday, when I was still inflight, he too had been overwhelmed with the question of whatever happened to me.

He told his fiancé about me and took her to his aunt's apartment to show her pictures of me when I was a wee baby. The migration story continued, but for now, I'll leave it at the point that he decided to move near me in British Columbia, where we went into business together in a move that totally rearranged my life in ways that were both painful and needful.

The Nashville Migration

Moving ahead four years, Kevin and I had parted ways and he moved back to Toronto. The business we started left me nearly a quarter million dollars in debt, and we shut it down. In this four-year period, I lost everything. Furthermore, I was reduced to sleeping on someone else's sofa and driving an old beat-up car that didn't belong to me.

One miserable night, I had a powerful dream that gave me hope. Something joyous was going off in me. In my dream, I saw a map, and on that map, there was a green dot somewhere around middle Tennessee. I had no other clues. I did what any rational person would do (say I, tongue-in-cheek): a short time later, I got in a car and drove down the West Coast to California, and then east towards Nashville.

I had no idea why I was there or what I would find, but I planned to stay until I knew. It was on that trip that I met a woman that I later proposed to, and we were married a few months later in January of 1986. Wanting to rebuild my life and make a difference in the world, I had grand dreams, but my path would take a direction I never would have imagined.

In early January, I was driving on Interstate 40 through Nashville before we were married. I realize that what I'm about to tell you spooks some people, but I would be dishonest to not tell you what really happened. As I was minding my own business, driving in traffic, the Holy Spirit drew my attention to a building on the right side with a man's name on it, and He said, "That's where you're going to work."

I was a little bit startled by this unsolicited input. After all, I wasn't praying. I wasn't asking God anything. I was just driving down the road. Then, to make matters worse, I saw copier logos on the side of the building, and I realized it was a copier dealer. I told God I absolutely never wanted to sell copiers again, but apparently, He had left the conversation.

I went to the building, found out that they were looking for a sales rep in Murfreesboro, and I got the job. I asked God to show me His ways to sell because I figured if He was directing me to that job, He could show me how to succeed in sales.

He was good with that request, and in an industry that averages a 25% closing rate, I averaged just over 90% and set a record for most sales while working less than my teammates and vacationing in Scotland.

At year's end, I was promoted to sales manager and began working in the very building God said I would work in. Things went pretty well there too. I led my team to a 430% increase year-over-year and was promoted to corporate trainer. In that position, I led a few coworkers to Christ and prospered in the process. Clearly God had His purpose in showing me that green dot on a map in my dream. Soon after, I became a U.S. citizen and life was looking very good. During our marriage, I had one more migration experience…

The Panama Migration

It was 2005 and I was in my living room reading and praying one morning. Then out of nowhere came another one of those mini-migration urges. This time I felt strongly that the Lord was inviting me to the nation of Panama. I had never been there, had no interest in going, and had never given it a thought. I didn't know anyone there or anyone who had ever been to Panama. There was simply no reason whatsoever I could think of to go there.

But that familiar tugging, that silent beckoning to destiny, was once again knocking on my heart's door. I told my wife, who was in the pool at the time, that I believed God was inviting us to Panama. She asked me, "Why?" I told her that when I asked Him that, it had something to do with finance and business. She asked me, "When?" I had already asked the Lord that question too, and He said to "make haste."

I did what any rational person would do who had some previous migration experience: I answered the call, booked the flights, and let my clients know I would be out of the country for a while.

One such client asked me when and why, and I gave him the same answers I had given my wife. He said, "Well, if you look for some real estate for me when you're down there, I'll underwrite the total cost of the trip for you both." I accepted, because at least that gave me a starting point. While there, I did find a large piece of beachfront property for him, and he put a $30 million offer on it. After that, I had no specific plans, so we headed inland to Boquete in the mountain region.

As I was headed to breakfast one morning, walking across the grassy, park-like property, the Lord spoke to me out of the blue again. This time He said, "Son, everything you need to know about business, you could learn in the rainforest." That's it. Nothing more. No explanation.

I went to the front desk to see if there was a business seminar being held in the rainforest. They looked at me strangely and said any seminars they would have, would be indoors. It was near the end of my trip, so I didn't get to explore much, but upon my return home, I googled to see if the words "business" and "rainforest" were in any way related. Turns out that the former CEO emeritus of Mitsubishi and another CEO had written a book called, *What We Learned in the Rainforest – Business Lessons From Nature.*

I learned that the rainforest was the most productive and diverse ecosystem on the planet, and I assumed that the topsoil must be rich, dark, and deep. Not so. It is shallow and acidic because the rain is constantly washing it away. That begged the question, "**How does God get abundance from scarcity?**"

I spent the next several years researching that question, returning to

Panama four times, gaining access to research papers from the Smithsonian World Headquarters for Tropical Research on Barro Colorado in the Panama Canal. I also traveled to Costa Rico, Belize, Barbados, Tobago, and the Upper Amazon region in South America, all in the quest to find the answer to that question. Those findings are in my book, *Rainforest Strategy*, with the foreword by Zig Ziglar.

The bottom line of this chapter is to encourage you to tune into those inner stirrings and take a chance to follow them. You and I don't know for sure how things will work out if you do take one of those mini migrations, but I can promise you two things… (1) It will definitely be an adventure you'll remember for the rest of your life, and... (2) If you don't step out and take flight, you will most likely never know what you missed out on.

My recommendation is to take the leap into the unknown. You'll survive, and it most likely will lead to a season of thriving you would never have known otherwise.

In the final chapter of this book, I'm going to share the most exhilarating content in this book. I literally get almost teared up when telling my wife about it. I've been looking forward to writing it since I started, but I knew it must be last.

So, turn to Chapter 17 and discover the 12 Unseen Laws of Guidance for YOUR JOURNEY …

CHAPTER 17

THE MYSTERY OF MIGRATION

Twelve Unseen Laws of Guidance For Your Journey

"God stirs the spirit before He moves your life."

Bird migration is so much more than a flock of birds heading south for the winter. It is one of the most remarkable miracles in the world. Creatures, many of them small enough to fit inside a teacup, cross vast oceans with no visible markers along the way. Tiny wings, held together with feathers, glide across mountain ranges with an ease that dwarfs our own abilities. Warblers weighing less than an ounce, terns no more than three ounces, cranes, and geese, to name only a few, follow invisible routes as precise as any commercial airliner, without the aid of maps, GPS, or mentor birds who have flown before them.

The heavens we behold with our eyes seem to be outlined with roads in the sky that only birds can see, and they all know how to navigate those roads. As you read through this final chapter, it may dawn upon you that everything we have covered so far has been in preparation for this moment. Design, dawn chorus, foraging, preening, lift, vigilance, synergy, trust, nesting, molting, and rest have all been leading here, to the mystery of guidance.

Birds have a built-in internal compass, not a physical organ, but a means nonetheless to navigate the heavens above with precision. We, on the other hand, carry the Spirit of God who knows all things and promises to guide us into all truth[1]. The same God who spoke the birds into existence and wrote migratory paths into instinct has written a sense of destiny, and eternity, into the human heart. We were never intended to walk through life aimlessly with no sense of direction, making things up as we go. He will guide us with precision, just as He guides the Arctic Tern from pole to pole and back.

The twelve laws I am about to share with you are not chiseled in stone. They are observable patterns woven into the wingbeats of birds and the steps of God's people. Each of these laws reveals a facet of how God leads, and shares a direct application for the assignment God has for you.

Law 1: The Inner Pull – When Destiny Stirs Before You Move
Before the first bird lifts its wings to head south for the winter, migration has already begun on the inside. It is the stirring of their inner clock that I discussed in the previous chapter. This stirring is so pronounced that German scientists have a word for it, "Zugunruhe," which simply means "migratory restlessness". They observed that even birds in captivity, as migration season draws near, become suddenly restless at night, hopping around in their cages, and vainly flapping their wings in an attempt to fly. It is as if their bones are made of iron and there is a giant magnet somewhere pulling on them, drawing them to take flight.

This happens despite no external changes in the environment, no change of weather, and food still being available. Yet something on the inside has awakened, and they must respond. God works like that with people.

Before your life gains movement,
your spirit begins to stir.

A job you once loved now lacks meaning. A business opportunity you seized in times past is yesterday's news. A city you were excited to call home now feels like an internment facility, walled in with no joy. In reality, nothing is wrong, but everything feels out of alignment.

It happens to all of us at one time or another. Philippians 1:6 tells us that God "who began a good work in you, will be faithful to complete it." Psalm 33:15 reminds us that God fashions our hearts individually, and I believe He places desires in our hearts for good things. Jeremiah said that God put a word in him that felt like a burning fire shut up in his bones[2]. Jeremiah did not conjure it up. God gave him that. Nehemiah said that God put it in his heart to rebuild the wall around Jerusalem. God is like that. He will put something in your heart. Will you recognize it, and will you follow through?

When your inner self begins to stir and restlessness becomes your reality, when you recognize that where you are and where you have been, may have been good but is not where God intends to leave you, pay close attention. You may have a case of Zugunruhe, the early tremors of destiny calling.

Law 2: Prepared Seasons – When Timing, Not Desire, Governs Movement – Restlessness is a potential indicator, but it's not enough to send a flock of birds south. Season sends a bird into the sky. There is a hormonal change that happens as days get shorter and temperatures recede. As winter approaches, food begins to thin. Prevailing winds change. These are the signals birds recognize as an approaching change of season, telling them, "It is time to leave."

Birds do not head off at random. They know when the season is right, and that's when they leave. Scripture tells us there is a time for every purpose under heaven. Psalm 1 reminds us that those who meditate in God's word will bring forth fruit *in its season*, not all at once, not every day, but in the right season. Paul tells us in Galatians 6:9 not to grow weary in well doing, for in *due season* we will reap if we do not lose heart. That is the interesting thing about God's sense of timing...

It is not partial. It is not based on sentimentality.
It is strategic, according to predetermined seasons.

In business, you may feel a transition coming, but things are not yet in place for it to happen. Don't worry. You may be receiving advance notice so you can prepare. The promised season will come. Doors will open. Relationships will form. Conditions will change.

Maybe what fed you well, no longer does. Don't panic. It may be time to move on. When the Brook Cherith dried up[3] (the very brook that sustained Elijah) God used that to tell him it was time to go to Zarephath, where flour and oil multiplied continuously until the drought ended.

To everything there is a season, including purpose, and all seasons are divinely orchestrated. Moving ahead of God's season for you is as risky as lagging behind it. Birds do not get anxious about the changing season. They wait until it comes, and whenever that is, they move. When desire and season converge, it's time to move.

Law 3: Invisible Pathways – Trusting the Road You Cannot See
The Arctic Tern is a striking white bird with what looks like a black ballcap on its head. Weighing only three ounces, this little guy will fly from the northern Arctic to southern Antarctica and back, every year of its life.

The thing is, there are no signs dangling from the clouds. No lane markers in the sky. No suspended billboards saying, "Turn right after Brazil." Yet their route is so consistent that scientists have mapped it with surprising precision. The big question is how.

God has prepared the heavens and the earth with guidance systems we scarcely comprehend. There are magnetic fields, wind corridors, star patterns, and polarized light that form invisible highways no human has ever seen, yet every migratory bird knows how to read them. That brings me to the third law of Heaven's Compass... Just because you can't see the path, doesn't mean it's not there.

Isaiah records the words of God...

> "I will lead the blind by ways they have not known. Along unfamiliar paths I will guide them."[4]

God led Israel through the Red Sea on a path that left no tracks, yet it was so real that an estimated three million men, women, and children walked between walls of water. Birds are not concerned about the lack of visible roads, or even the absence of landmarks when flying over the ocean. They trust the compass God placed within them. You can learn to do the same. Purpose is a preplanned path that God has embedded in your heart.

You don't invent your
purpose, you discover it.

Your job is to seek it out and align with it, not manufacture it out of whole cloth. That turns faith into discovery of God's intentions for you, rather than constructing what you want God's intentions to be.

Law 4: Multi Layered Guidance – How God Confirms His Leading – If birds only had one compass to rely on, a single overcast day could end their journey permanently. Fortunately, God has not left them so vulnerable. They navigate by the sun when available. At night they are guided by the stars, but only if the sky is clear. When the sun is hidden, they can be guided by polarized light. They always have access to magnetic fields, and when flying over land, they can use landmarks and even scent along familiar coasts. It is redundancy by design. If one system fails, another still works.

The good news is that God leads His own in multiple ways as well. Maybe something new has stirred in your heart. Then, as you read Scripture, a verse jumps out at you, amplifying that stirring. Maybe a trusted voice reaches out, unaware of your stirring, and offers counsel that confirms what you have been sensing. Then circumstances align, and to top it off, a peace settles over the entire decision. Paul tells us in 2 Corinthians 13:1,

> "By the mouth of two or three witnesses every word shall be established."

Sometimes those witnesses come from His Word. Sometimes from the Holy Spirit. Trusted counselors speak into your life. Circumstances line up like dominoes, ready to set in motion a chain reaction that makes a way for you.

When you get one signal, ask God for others to confirm. Birds trust more than one compass. It would be wise if we did the same. God has directed me through a single word on many occasions, but that word was so strong and clear it left no doubt. When it feels more like a tug or a hunch, seek more confirmation.

Caution: A series of circumstantial "coincidences" may only be what is known as "confirmation bias" where we give meaning to unrelated events to support a hoped-for conclusion. Always ask the Lord to guide your thinking and choices by His peace.

Law 5: Strength Before Journey – How God Equips You in Advance – There is a cute little bird weighing little more than a heavy paperclip called the Blackpoll Warbler. Before it launches across the Atlantic Ocean, it enters a hot dog eating contest at Coney Island. Well, not really, but it does gorge on insects and seeds, nearly doubling its weight. Fat gets stored under its skin. The muscles it needs to fly, thicken and strengthen, while its digestive system shrinks to reduce unneeded weight. Even its blood chemistry adjusts to maximize endurance.

Before it takes off on this extraordinary 3,600-mile flight, first achieved by man in 1927 thanks to Charles Lindbergh, the Blackpoll Warbler undergoes an overhaul, a refitting, a God designed remodel, converting basic provision into a powerhouse, capable of a multi-day transoceanic flight. Once that transformation is complete, and not until then, it rises into the night sky to track the stars and cross the ocean.

Ephesians 2:10 says that you are God's workmanship, created in Christ Jesus for good works that He prepared in advance for you to walk in. Hebrews 13:21 is a prayer that God would equip you with everything good for doing His will. When Moses complained that he did not speak well enough to accomplish his assignment, God told him, "I will help you speak and teach you what to say."[5]

The paths you have come through, the skills you have acquired, the disciplines you have adopted, and the character you have forged when no one was looking will all come into play. None of it will be wasted. The job you did not want, may have trained you for the business you have always wanted.

Birds never undertake their mission on an empty stomach. They allow God's preparation regimen to do its work. When you start thinking about what you may need for the next phase of your life, look back and consider what God has already brought you through and deposited in you. You may discover that what looked random was, in fact, carefully choreographed training flights.

Law 6: The Courageous Launch – When Obedience Sets Miracles in Motion – At some point, preparation must result in commitment. Remember the Bar tailed Godwit? Talk about committing to something. After it gathers with friends and family in early autumn for one last time to eat and eat and eat, nearly doubling its weight, it then shrinks its digestive organs and enlarges its flight muscles in advance of its migration to breeding grounds in New Zealand and Australia.

That is a big trip, but here's the kicker. Once it commits and gets in the air, there is no turning back and there is no place to land until it completes the journey, some seven to eleven days later. No more food. No rest. It's a nonstop flight, the first migration for some. How do they know where New Zealand is, especially with no landmarks? It seems that once they start, the miracle of guidance begins to unfold.

When Joshua led Israel to the flatlands where the Jordan River was in flood stage, the river did not welcome them and part. It remained swift and daunting until the priests' feet stepped into the water as they carried the Ark of the Covenant. Only then did the miracle unfold, and the Jordan stood still.

Ten lepers approached Jesus for healing. He told them to go show themselves to the priests. As they went, they were healed. Abraham is another example. God told him to go to a land He would show him. In effect, God was saying, "Head north. I will guide you along the way and let you know when you are in the right place." That is a lot like migration. In each case, obedience initiates the miracle.

There comes a point when further analysis and preparation is no longer prudence, but fear dressed up as caution. Every migration begins with a single act of courage and a decision that there will be no turning back.

Law 7: Energy Flow and Wind Riding – Partnering with God's Momentum – If migration depended solely on frantic flapping, many birds would expire early in the journey. Scientists observing birds in migration note that when birds are in migration mode, their flight appears quite leisurely. That's because they have learned to cooperate with the environment rather than try to overpower it.

Different species do this in different ways. Hawks spiral upward on a thermal, using columns of warm air to lift them high without flapping.

Geese time their journey to catch tailwinds that carry them farther with greater ease. Some species find corridors in the jet stream and glide for hours on high-speed upper-level winds.

The one thing in common is this. They have learned to ride the invisible gift of God, the wind beneath their wings. Think of the wind of the Spirit. In Galatians 5:25, Paul tells us, "Since we live by the Spirit, let us keep in step with the Spirit."

God promises those who wait on the Lord, will mount up with wings like eagles and will not grow weary[6]. Paul told the Corinthian church that a great and effective door had been opened to him in Ephesus[7]. He did not knock the door down. He did not create the door. It had been opened to him. His role was to discern it and walk through it.

In your work and business life, there will be times when you sense an unexpected ease that feels like the wind of favor. Maybe it is an unexpected inquiry, a new opportunity, or an introduction to someone.

These are doors that open with unusual ease. Confirm with the Lord if it is from Him. If you still have peace, then proceed. Do not mistake fear for God's leading to not do something. There will always be unanswered questions. Faith moves anyway.

Law 8: Formation Flight – Why Some Flights Require a Flock
I have already talked about the "V" formation slicing through the sky courtesy of a flock of southbound geese. They are a masterclass of physics in motion and a community united in action. Their flight pattern allows those behind to fly with greater ease and speed. They alternate leaders to maintain that efficiency, and in so doing, they travel as much as seventy percent farther than if they flew alone.

Your mission may include distances God never intended you to cross by yourself, goals that are too big for one person to handle. The person who insists on being a one-man operation builds limits into his life. The high achiever becomes a bottleneck if he refuses help when it is needed. Ecclesiastes reminds us that two are better than one because they will have a good reward for their labor. If one falls, the other will lift him up[8]. The early church exploded across Asia Minor and throughout the Roman Empire not just because of Paul, but also because of the supporting work of a network of home churches.

God's leading will include times when you need to fly in formation with others to reach the goal. That does not mean there will not be plenty of moments when you are flying solo. You will experience wilderness moments and solitary nights of wrestling with God. But the long migrations, the big hairy audacious goals, often require a flock. In that flock there are mentors ahead of you, peers alongside you, those you are mentoring behind you, and intercessors beneath you. Some distances cannot be crossed any other way.

Law 9: Course Correction – When Storms and Detours Don't Destroy Destiny – As wondrous as migration is, it is rarely without challenges. Storms have been known to knock flocks hundreds of miles off course. Unexpected cold fronts have pinned birds to the ground. Sometimes the youngest migrants misread a cue and end up somewhere not on the original plan. Regardless of setbacks, they eventually find their way.

Just because a flock got pushed westward instead of southward does not nullify the inward compass. Birds knocked off course regroup, reorient, and resume their journey, undaunted. Scientists are thrilled when they see birds outside their normal range. They call them vagrants who, despite being in unfamiliar terrain, will still forage, find shelter, and eventually continue on their migration. When you see a bird knocked off course, temporarily finding food and shelter in a nearby marsh, that is not failure. It is a testimony of God's ingenuity and redemption.

My journey, perhaps like yours, has included ferocious, life altering storms, many of them of my own making, and some unnecessary detours. I was blown off course at times, drawn off course on other occasions, pursuing what turned out to be a draining distraction instead of the enriching opportunity someone promised, and I naively believed.

You may have had a major health crisis that sidelined you, a business failure, or a failed marriage. Most likely you have made decisions you now regret. And because you blame yourself, you believe you have ruined God's plan for your life. If poor choices disqualified destiny, David would never have become king, nor would Moses have led Israel out of Egypt. Solomon reminds us,

> "Though the righteous fall seven times, they rise again."[9]

Maybe he learned that from his father David, who wrote...

> "The steps of a good man are ordered by the Lord, and He delights in his way. Though he fall, he shall not be utterly cast down, for the Lord upholds him with His hand."[10]

Jonah deliberately fled in the opposite direction of what he knew to be God's will, yet his mission to Nineveh was still waiting when he was ready to obey.

Your destiny is not as fragile as you may assume. Your mistakes were never a surprise to God. He gave you His promises knowing when and where you would slip, yet He still called you. Romans 11:29 tells us that the gifts and callings of God are irrevocable.

The Holy Spirit acts as a Heavenly Compass within you, making allowance for correction when needed, and can reorient you from any place on the map. As beneficial as it is, to never get knocked off course, the important thing is learning to respond to the nudge leading you back to the path God has prepared for you. Birds do not waste time on self-condemnation. That is a uniquely human trait. Birds adjust and resume. We are invited to do the same.

Law 10: Providence on the Path – How Provision Meets Obedience – Sandhill Cranes abound where I live, claiming the lake across the street as their own. They are magnificent in flight, but watching them land in shallow water is its own spectacle as their legs unfold like delicate landing gear. The water is teeming with their favorite fish, though their preference is lizards, frogs, berries, and insects. It is as if the table was set for them, with all their preferred foods waiting for their arrival.

In a very real sense, that is true. Before they ever left the northlands, rain was filling the ponds and lakes they would later visit. Plants were growing and preparing a harvest of seeds, grains, and berries. Lizards were multiplying, much to my wife's displeasure. Then, when things are in place down south, winds up north shift and invite them down for a feast. Cranes don't arrive with a "will work for food" sign. They come expecting abundance, and year after year that is exactly what they find.

Abraham experienced that on Mount Moriah. At God's command, he took Isaac up the mountain to sacrifice. When Isaac asked where the lamb was, Abraham said, "God will provide for Himself the lamb for a burnt offering."[11] Only after he climbed the mountain, stacked the wood, and prepared the fire did an angel stop him, and a ram appeared, caught in a thicket.

Elijah was fed by ravens twice daily, but not at any random spot. He was told to go to the Brook Cherith. Once he got there, and only then, did the ravens began their DoorDash delivery service[12]. Jesus used birds to illustrate that God feeds them in the places their obedience to design and instinct takes them.

The tenth law is this. Provision meets you where obedience leads you. The resources you need are not stored in the place of comfort. They are prepared in the place of calling. The customers you are meant to serve are lining up around the problem you are designed to solve. Go there. To be clear, I am not suggesting you abandon wisdom or planning. Those matter.

When God invites you to a new horizon, you can rest assured He has already laid up provision along the way.

Law 11: The Promise of Return – How Journeys Transform You
Young warblers that have just left the security of the forest for the first time to answer the call for something greater are like the young entrepreneur who has just left the security of a well-paying job. Its wings are functional but only tested in controlled environments. What lies beyond the forest is largely unknown.

Several months later, when that same warbler returns, it is a different bird. It has dodged storms, evaded predators, and found food in unfamiliar places. It returns with a mental map of landmarks and coastlines and knows how to read and ride the wind like an experienced sailor. Its body has gained muscle. Its instincts are razor sharp. The route it will take next time is now etched not only in instinct, but in experience.

The journeys God takes us on have similar implications. God promised to restore His people after their long exile in Egypt. Job came out of his dark trial with a deeper revelation of God and received a double portion. Jesus Himself went into the wilderness by the leading of the Spirit and emerged in the power of the Spirit.

The purpose of migration is more than giving birds a warm climate. The migratory process is a school. God matures them in ways staying home never could. See the big assignments that God gives you as mini migrations. Starting a family, starting a business, building a team, building a following. When you accept God's invitation to a new horizon, you will not only get through it, you'll also be changed by it.

The eleventh law of Heaven's Compass is that every journey initiated by God brings clarity, greater strength, and a more certain sense of identity. You begin as one person and return as another, the same but different, more aligned with the person God designed you to be.

Law 12: Eternity in the Heart – The Compass Within – This may be the deepest mystery of all. What, in the end, really guides the bird? Scientists have documented magnetite particles in their beaks that are sensitive to the Earth's magnetic field. They have identified proteins in their eyes that respond to polarized light.

But none of those things fully explain the longing awakened inside the bird, strong enough to draw it thousands of miles from home to a specific place, perhaps on a remote island, where it will meet others, find a mate, and breed. Somehow, something in the heart of the bird recognizes home, even if it has never seen it before.

Ecclesiastes 3:11 says that God has put eternity in our hearts. Some call it a God shaped void. Using the bird analogy, it's as if He put magnetite in our hearts tuned to God Himself. When I was about 8 or 9 years old, I wanted to know God. I went door to door asking people if they knew Him so I could learn about Him. No one knew. As a young teen, I wanted connection with Him but did not know how to reach Him. I assumed He could hear me, so I would tell Him jokes I thought were funny. My inner "spiritual magnetite" was trying to find Him.

Romans 8 tells us that as many as are led by the Spirit of God, these are the children of God[13]. In Colossians, Paul instructs us to let the peace of God act as an umpire in our hearts[14] to help us make decisions. Jesus added that the Spirit of Truth would guide us into all truth[15]. The

Holy Spirit within us is our compass, not only for daily life, but for our eternal home.

You have been there. So have I... when things change quickly, sometimes destructively. Friends leave. Markets shift. Partnerships dissolve. Business ventures take a nosedive. Yet if you listen closely, if you shut out the noise of the drama playing out in front of you, you will rediscover the quiet welcoming draw of the Holy Spirit toward the purposes of God for your life. It never goes away. You can ignore it, deny it, refuse it outright, but it remains.

As you mature in Christ and grow in relationship with Him, you will more readily recognize the "yes" that comes with peace, and the "no" that comes with the absence of peace. You will become better able to navigate the migrations of life as aptly as any bird.

We tend to rely on navigation tools like spreadsheets, algorithms, market research, and the opinion of our barber. Those tools can be useful, but your true north is internal. Your destiny is not just mapped in the sky above. It is written in your heart.

The Bigger Picture

Migration began this journey with the first bird in a mist covered marsh, lifting its head under a diamond studded night sky, sensing something it could not see, but would not deny. That sensing turned to restlessness, leading to seasons transitioning, invisible paths beckoning, multiple compasses aligning, bodies getting stronger, wings spreading to catch the air, unified flocks forming, storms weathered, detours corrected, fields and marshes found that were prepared for their arrival, and at last, a return home, transformed.

As fascinating as migration is, it is not really about birds. As I have said all along, it is about the God who designed and programmed them, who also designed you and me and gave us a tremendous operating system, unmatched by anything on God's green earth. If He can guide a tiny hummingbird across the Gulf of America nonstop, to arrive at a place it has never been, to feast on flowers it has never seen but somehow knew would be there, He can safely and certainly guide you through any transition to arrive at any horizon in life.

If He can sustain a Bar tailed Godwit on a nonstop transoceanic flight, I am confident He can sustain us through whatever season we are in now. If God can lead cranes in great spirals, guiding them across continents and arriving within days of the same time, year after year, I feel good about the likelihood of Him guiding us to relationships and opportunities at the right time. If God can whisper to the tiny warbler, giving it instincts to navigate by star maps, surely, He can whisper strategy and direction into our hearts.

If God is sending you, He will sustain you. Where God guides, He provides. Where He calls, He equips. Where He directs, He protects until your time on earth has come to an end. Where He stirs you to go, He goes with you. He will never leave you nor forsake you[16].

You are not left to wander aimlessly through a hostile environment, hoping to make it another day, and maybe, if you are lucky, find some purpose. You came into this world with an inner desire to connect with God, find your bearings, and migrate through life under the guidance of the Divine Compass, the Holy Spirit, along a path He marked out for you before the foundations of the world.

This is still a hostile environment. Some nights will be dark. Some days will be stormy and knock you off course. There will be times when you feel grounded or set aside, even alone, as you wait for new feathers of destiny to grow. And there will also be exhilarating days when you can scarcely catch your breath, standing in awe of unexpected favor and goodness, soaring on a thermal you did not see coming.

No matter the situation, there will always be that steady homing device within, calling you back to God, to experience His love, to walk in His kindness, and to know Him better than you know yourself. I urge you now, despite turmoil and uncertainty, spread your wings and catch the wind of the Spirit. Trust that "pull" from within, and fly the path of destiny God has laid out for you.

The journey will be interesting, to say the least. There will be adventure and stories to tell your grandchildren. And you will arrive, not because you had it all figured out, and certainly not because you executed flawlessly, but because the One who calls you is faithful to complete what He began in you[17].

Every surrendered soul to the purposes of God, like every determined migrating bird, eventually reaches the place prepared for it. Jesus told His followers,

> "I go and prepare a place for you, and if I go and prepare a place for you, I will come again and receive you to Myself, that where I am, there you may be also.[18]"

That is the true story of migration. God has prepared an eternal destination for anyone who believes in Him[19]. The invitation is open to all.

When the silver cord is loosed[20] and your journey takes you home, you will look back in amazement at the storms you survived, the winds that gave you lift, the detours that protected you, and the seasons that transformed you. And you will, in awe, whisper, "He was guiding me the whole way."

For the secret life of birds is the testimony of creation to a God who leads you with immeasurable love, provides for you with tender purpose, and carries you on the winds of grace into the destiny He planned for you before you were born. So,

Spread your wings. Your sky awaits.

The mini migrations are great tutors, but the eternal migration is one you do not want to miss. He does not want you to miss it either. That is why He put that longing in your heart, and His offer still stands.

I hope you will say yes to Him and be on the epic migration of all migrations, coming sooner than you may expect.

The End

References: 1) John 16:13 2) Jeremiah 20:9 3) 1 Kings 17:7. 4) Isaiah 42:16. 5) Exodus 4:12. 6) Isaiah 40:31 7) 1 Corinthians 16:9 8) Ecclesiastes 4:9-12. 9) Proverbs 24:16 10) Psalm 37:23-24. 11) Genesis 22:8 12) 12) 1 Kings 17:2-7 13) Romans 8:13 14) Colossians 3:15 15) John 16:13. 16) Hebrews 13:5 17) Philippians 1:6 18) John 14:3 19) John 3:16 20) Ecclesiastes 12:6

www.ingramcontent.com/pod-product-compliance
Lightning Source LLC
LaVergne TN
LVHW010056110826
845155LV00028B/360

* 9 7 8 1 8 7 7 9 9 4 0 7 4 *